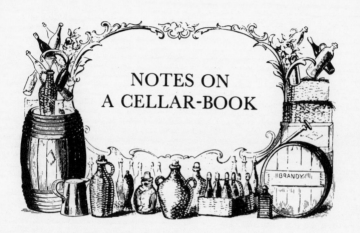

NOTES ON
A CELLAR-BOOK

George Saintsbury
A portrait by Sir William Nicholson in Merton College, Oxford.

NOTES ON A
CELLAR-BOOK

BY

GEORGE SAINTSBURY

WITH A NEW PREFACE BY
H. W. YOXALL

MAYFLOWER BOOKS

TO
R. K.
ONE OF THE BEST OF FELLOWS
THE BEST POET AND TALETELLER OF HIS
GENERATION
AND ONE THAN WHOM
NO LIVING ENGLISHMAN
HAS DONE MORE TO FOSTER THE SPIRIT
THAT WON IN 1914–18
I OFFER
THIS MY FIRST AND LAST DEDICATION
IN PLACE OF
THE MANY REVIEWS AND THE MANY BOTTLES
OF WHICH
BY SOME CANTRIP OF FORTUNE
IT HAS NEVER BEEN MY LOT OR LUCK
DURING SOME THIRTY YEARS ACQUAINTANCE
TO OFFER HIM
ONE

G. S.
(Bath, *Easter*, 1920)

CONTENTS

PREFACE TO THE SECOND REISSUE

WHEN, nearly sixty years ago, *Notes on a Cellar-Book* first appeared it rapidly ran through four reprints. The author, previously known only in academic circles, suddenly became the cult-figure of a new field of scholarship—oenophily. His book inspired a flow of others on the aesthetic appreciation of wine, and of gastronomic memoirs. A dining club was founded in his name, with at best his grudging consent and entirely without his participation; it still flourishes, and admission thereto is eagerly sought by wine lovers. On the death of the Professor a delegation of the club went to Bath, with a magnificent wreath to honour his interment—only to find that this was taking place in Southampton, so that their pious gesture unfortunately miscarried. Saintsbury was difficult even to the end.

The book, if the publishers will permit me to record this, had soon been allowed to go out of print; but for students of wine it was already established as a kind of testament of their faith, and second-hand copies went to a premium. I was living abroad when it first appeared, and the 1923 edition, which I acquired over fifty years ago in the Charing Cross Road, cost me double the published price.

For many years the *Notes* remained a legendary influence. Saintsbury-worship prevailed; the author, who had confessed his personal service of Dionysus, became himself a kind of modern god of wine.

Then the whirligig of time brought its revenge. In the 1950s mutterings of dissent began to be heard; the idol was rumoured to have feet of clay. His High Tory politics, which to some extent obtrude upon the book, became unpopular in a period of incipient egalitarianism. Some ten years ago a man who certainly knows wine published, in a reputable magazine, a violent attack on Saintsbury as a writer in general and on the *Notes* in particular. He asserted that the Professor was a clumsy stylist, that his book ignored the sciences of viticulture and vinification, that its contents were both incomplete and out of date, and that it was the work of a *gourmand*, not a *gourmet*.

With the first part of this arraignment I must to some extent concur. It continues to surprise me that a man who was a Regius Professor of Rhetoric, who knew all fine western literature and could recite much of it by heart, who had even published *The History of English Prose Rhythm*, should write so turgidly, with so many periphrases and parentheses, so many superfluous literary allusions—the last of which annoy me more, perhaps, because I can only recognise about half of them. I cannot honestly recommend the *Notes* as a model of English prose style. But do not let that put you off.

For against the other accusations I must protest. The book is meant to be personal and occasional, not historical and comprehensive. Saintsbury specifically says that he had been asked to write a *History of Wine*, but that he 'could not fully entertain the idea.' Instead, he offered a slight series of reminiscences of his own purchases and consumption, based on the notes he had kept, from 1884 to 1915, in an 'ordinary exercise book, cloth-backed, with mottled sideboards outside, and unruled leaves within.' It was begun at one end in his West Kensington days, then turned over and continued from the other end in Edinburgh. The actual book, incidentally, with its entries in the Professor's almost illegible writing, was sold some twenty years ago at Christie's for £300, resold by the purchaser, an antiquarian bookseller, to an enthusiastic *amateur*, and in the autumn of 1977, now handsomely cased in leather, was offered again at auction and fetched £1,550.

Thus Saintsbury never intended to write the kind of book he is accused of not writing. There was no cause for him, though he has been attacked for this, to do more than touch on the plagues of oidium and phylloxera that ravaged the vineyards in his middle age; he had almost exclusively drunk older vintages unaffected by these infestations. Was he too narrow? Apart from fortified wines he drank mostly French *crus*, so he mostly wrote about them. Admittedly he was weak on German wine (as are many knowledgeable wine-lovers still), and the few odd bottles that he bought from other countries naturally earned only passing references, since he wrote many years before the table wines of Italy, Spain and Portugal—and California—reached their present standards.

If port, champagne, claret and burgundy occupy a greater proportion of his reminiscences than they would in a general wine book, this is for the sufficient reason that the greater proportion of his drinking was devoted to them. Even on the subject of claret our critic charges him with slighting St-Emilion and totally neglecting Pomerol, but these areas were little known and less sold in Britain in his time. An unenthusiastic reference to the famous Cheval Blanc has been fastened on; but the first really great vintage of this château was made in the year after he had completed his manuscript. If we are distressed by his apparent injustice to the wines of the Loire we should recall that their preferment also dates from after his time.

Again, he has been criticised by wine purists for devoting nearly half of his book to beer and spirits. But in his day gentlemen bought beer by the cask and spirits by the case, and kept them in their cellars. These drinks—beer not ignoble and spirits certainly noble—justified the attention in his *Notes on a Cellar-Book* that their presence in his

cellar demanded. I am in fact rather touched by
the consideration he gave to gin and rum
particularly—drinks ever popular indeed, but
rarely accorded such serious attention as they
deserve.

As to the reproach of *gourmandise*, the menus
that he prints are certainly for the most part long
meals, and in 1919 he confessed that some of them
seemed over-elaborate. But meals *were* long in
that period of entertaining; two world wars have
shrunk our stomachs, and shortage of service has
shortened our menus. But I think his critics on
these grounds do not realise that servings then
were very small, in comparison with the gargan-
tuan portions now dispensed in most restaurants;
also that one was not compelled to take both the
John Dory and the *fillets de saumon*, both the
chaudfroid de volaille and the *vol-au-vent financière*,
both turkey and blackcock.

Nevertheless the order of his menus is somewhat surprising to modern taste: a *mayonnaise
de homard* after the haunch of mutton seems
unnecessary when two fish dishes had been
offered before. And one queries his insertion of
champagne after Montilla, Johannisberger and
Château Grillet, and before a burgundy and a
claret, with the old burgundy preceding a comparatively young, and lighter, claret. I should
not, as the Professor did, serve a 22-year-old
Château Lafite with *canapés d'anchois*, even though
these were *au fromage*. But the ordering of wine
lists and their marriage to menus are a legitimate
field for experiment. A contemporary connoi-

sseur, a true connoisseur, commends red wine with anchovies. We are perhaps too hidebound now in our selections and arrangements. I must, in general, accept the Professor's judgement, because he certainly knew the character of each bin in his cellar. One is impressed by the fact that his favourites are still the great names of today.

Again, where we dare to disagree, we must allow for the fact that the character of many *châteaux* and *domaines* has been changed, in our time, by modern methods of vinification. These are supposed to correspond with contemporary taste but have in fact been more influenced by economic circumstances. The vintner cannot now afford to make a wine requiring much time to develop and still offer it at a price that buyers of ordinary means can afford. We drink much wine too soon. It is good to be reminded of *vins de garde* and the *méthode ancienne*. One must remember that Saintsbury's salary as a Regius Professor was £600 a year; but he recalls that in his earlier days any man 'with a few hundreds a year' would be expected to house at least a modest cellar. And he, with his six hundreds and his literary fees, could assemble one, not very large indeed, but of magnificent quality and full maturity.

Now that the unpleasant question of money has arisen I may confess to a slight amusement at Saintsbury's complaints about the exorbitant cost of wine during the later years of his record; how, today, would one rush to purchase at prices that he deplores, in 1919, as being 'abnormal and preposterous.' On the other hand I am grieved at the thought of a man who loved it so much being taken off wine, so long before his death, by doctors who lacked the pharmacological knowledge and resources of their successors. Saintsbury spent the last eighteen years of his life, not in complete abstention, but largely without the solace he loved so much. Was this necessary? Is great old age worth achieving on such terms?

His fulminations against those whom he called by the then current slang name of Pussyfoots are now happily outdated; the horrible results of the American experiment with Prohibition have removed that threat. Today the attention of kill-joys has been diverted from the pleasures of alcohol to those of nicotine—and Saintsbury enjoyed a good cigar.

Though he was a generous drinker, he, like all true lovers of wine, was never excessive. Students of his whom I have met, who knew him at the end of his Edinburgh career, spoke of him as genial and mellow at the end of his long dinners; but, as he says, he never saw 'guests under the table,' and was certainly never there himself. One should remember, too, in considering his formidable wine lists, that no aperitifs were served before those meals.

As to the character of our author, I never met him, and have to rely on the testimony of those pupils, now themselves grown old if not already dead, and of his correspondents. They tell of a man quirky, perhaps, and sometimes gruff, though of a general pleasant dry humour; very much what people call 'a character;' but always kind and generous to any youngster who showed an interest in any of his interests. And does not this personality emerge from every page of the *Notes*? He speaks of a favourite Hermitage as the manliest wine he ever knew; is he not the manliest of authors? (It was against this Hermitage, by the way, that the cellar-book carries the annotation 'The wine that made RLS walk that night to Dulwich.' This, naturally, is in the London pages. I have never seen this quoted anywhere, but few have seen the actual cellar-book, in contrast with the many thousands who have read the *Notes*.) As to the humour, read pages 127–8 of this volume, and the incident of the parlour-maid and the three decanters.

So, to summarise, this small book is not—it could not be—a general guide to wine drinking today, though all he wrote can be applied, *mutatis mutandis*, to our own experiences. It is however a seminal volume that should be in the library of every wine lover. It deepens our comprehension of books by his admirers: André Simon, Warner Allen, Maurice Healy, and others. It gives the picture of a man who really loved wine—indeed who loved most alcoholic drinks—who reflected about them deeply and expressed what he felt with nice epithets and revealing analogies. It provides an inspiration for every *amateur* to experiment widely, to meditate on his potations, to form individual judgements unbiased by the *clichés* of general opinion. We should always remember Saintsbury's statement, 'I have never yet given a second-hand opinion of anything.'

I have been a student of wine for over half a century. The more I study it, the more grateful I am for having come early on Saintsbury's book, to inspire me with a sense of this necessity of personal judgement and to discourage dogmatism on any aspect of this ever-changing but ever-gratifying field of research. So I end with his great affirmation, that wine 'pleased my senses, cheered my spirits, improved my moral and intellectual powers, besides enabling me to confer the same benefits on other people.' There is his motive; there you have, in short, the justification of this book, now happily once more available.

H. W. YOXALL

PREFACE TO THE REISSUE

I suppose most men who love books have an actual or a mental shelf of favourite indispensables which have been read and dipped into so often that they have become an integral part of their owners' lives. My own includes White's *Selborne*, *The Wind in the Willows*, *War and Peace*, *Vanity Fair*, *Vice Versa*, *Alice*, and a lot of Lear.

For many of us that is the shelf to which Saintsbury's *Notes on a Cellar-Book* already belongs.

No-one who loves good wine and enjoys talking about it (which has always been a large part of the fun) can consider himself to have been properly educated unless he has sipped the wisdom in these pages, savoured the bouquet of the anecdotes and relished to the full the after-taste of the footnotes.

For those who have already done so and who browse again from time to time it would be presumptuous in me to suppose that I can add anything. This preface is therefore written with those in mind for whom the pleasure (comparable perhaps to the first sip of a first growth of a superlative year?) lies ahead.

First let us be clear what sort of book this is and is not. It is something in the nature of a piece of rich embroidery for which the canvas-backing was 'an ordinary exercise book . . . with mottled paper sideboards outside and unruled leaves within' in which the author listed the wines in his cellar.

It is not one of those 'how to do it' books.

Urbane, leisurely, splendidly personal and enthusiastic, remarkably catholic, and the work of a man of vast erudition, it contents itself with offering advice, as sound today as it was in 1920, on 'how it may be done'.

Secondly, how should it be read?

To enjoy it to the full I have found that the author's hints on how to drink port may conveniently guide us in this matter also: 'A trial of the bouquet; a slow sip; a rather larger and slightly less slow one, and so on; but *never a gulp*'.

Two customs in particular which are described in these notes stand out as being different from those of today: the age at which wine was drunk, and the way in which, while before-dinner drinking is hardly mentioned, after-dinner drinking not only of port or liqueurs but specially of claret was a major feature of the evening.

On the first point, the age of wine, we are the victims of the warlike period through which we have passed in the last half-century. Nothing can be done about it so it is not worth wasting time in regret. In any case not only the customs but in some cases the wines themselves have changed. Vintage port is still made as it was in Professor Saintsbury's lifetime and, given good years in Portugal, generous godfathers in England and parents with iron self-control, there is no reason why boys born in this decade should not be sipping the vintages of the sixties when they come to man's estate in the eighties and nineties; but burgundies and claret are for the most part purposely made as lighter wines today so that the remarks in this book about the age of these wines generally refer to wines which were differently constituted.

Of the present-day habit of drinking strong waters on an empty stomach before dinner, rather than wine on a full one afterwards, it is hard to believe that the author would have approved, for all his tolerance and breadth of mind. He only mentions the word 'cocktail' once, in connection with transatlantic whisky (about which he is not very kind); but, since he is referring to a straight drink and not a mixed one, he is obviously using the word in a different sense.

He takes little interest in what may be drunk before dinner and no cognizance whatever of what an old Frenchwoman of my acquaintance used to call '*ces horribles apéritifs américains*'.

(Mercifully this lady died before her granddaughter made her *début* and adopted the then fashionable Parisian habit of swigging '*Scotch-on-the-Rocks*' before luncheon.)

It might be argued that since the customs

described are in some cases different, the advice offered is out of date.

To this I would reply: 'Nonsense!'

Much wine is now being enjoyed by more English men and women than ever before, not as something special but as a regular good habit. Many who started—and you must start somewhere—by ordering bottles which were at any rate labelled 'Beaujolais' or 'Pouilly-Fuissé' or 'Liebfraumilch' (whatever that may mean) have already been experimenting for years, far beyond these wholesome teething beverages. They realize that there are subtleties and grandeurs which do not reveal themselves to a palate which has been marinaded before dinner in a mixture of raw spirit, ingeniously advertised distillations, and tobacco-smoke.

They are a growing company and for them this book will be a storehouse of inspiration.

Just to titillate the palate let me end by making a very few quotations:—

Why not, for instance, manzanilla in large tall beakers with oysters? Professor Saintsbury can 'strongly recommend the practice.'

Specially in these days of high prices for clarets which bear great names, why not cultivate a closer acquaintance with the good *premiers bourgeois*? 'Some such wines will turn out just as well as any but the best classed growths'.

Why not, instead of risking the rigours of the ice-bucket or the refrigerator, try the Professor's method of cooling champagne? I myself have been doing it for years. It 'gives all the coolness necessary and does not "numb the ethers".'

In his *Conclusio ad diversos*, the author names a few of the things which it is good to have done. Let me make an addition.

It is good—very good—to have sipped and savoured the Saintsbury 1920, but it's even better to have the privilege of offering it now, lying in its cradle with its honourable cobwebs, in perfect condition as a vintage book to be enjoyed by a whole new generation of appreciative people.

ANDREW GRAHAM

PRELIMINARY

THE old joke 'Who has tied my son to this sword?'
may occur to some in respect of any prefatory
matter to so very little a book as this is likely to be;
but perhaps it may be possible to make it a not
quite superfluous part of the book itself. Not
improbable and welcome readers of it may know
that, in a larger and more serious work[1] some time
ago, while disclaiming the intention of trespassing
further on shelf-room and public time, I mentioned that I had been asked for, and had actually
begun, a *History of Wine*, and that, if circumstances had been more favourable, I should have
liked to resume it. Rather to my surprise the hint
was jumped at, and not only private but public,
and (if I may coin a word in the manner in which
I have often of old shocked purist ears) even
'publisherial' requests reached me. I felt the
compliment, but could not fully entertain the

---

[1] *History of the French Novel,* vol. ii, Preface.

idea. There would have been a considerable literature to look up; and while I was not favourably situated in respect of access to it, my original farewell had been no trick, but the result of a genuine sense that I was getting too old for such a work. It would need infinite research to satisfy my own ideas of thoroughness: for I have never yet given a second-hand opinion of any thing, or book, or person. Also, I should have had to drink more good wine than would now be good for my pocket or perhaps even my health, and more bad than I could contemplate without dismay in my advancing years. So I resisted, not indeed the devil (who for the best of reasons hates wine), but these too amiable angels, as to any exhaustive treatment of the subject.

It did not, however, seem to me that there was anything inconsistent with what I had said in committing to paper certain notes and reminiscences on that subject which might amuse some readers, be profitable to others if things go well, and, whether they go well or ill, add a little to the literature of one of the three great joys of life. A man must have a mighty conceit of himself if he thinks that he can add much worth adding to what has been already written of Women and Song. But except in song itself (wherein, alas, I have but critical and not creative skill), and in ways rather general than particular, I must say I think Wine has been stinted of its due literary sizings. There are noble exceptions, Thackeray perhaps the greatest of them. But the serious books on wine have, as a rule, been rather dull, and the non-serious books and even passages not very 'ingoing.' I have known a most virtuous person, a true wine-lover and a man of great talent, speak in prose of 'Carte Blanche' (or no matter what colour) as if it were a kind of champagne like *brut* or *œil de perdrix*; and even the minor singers—I do not speak of Panard or Tom Brown, who are not here 'minor,' of Peacock or Thackeray himself—are apt to be vague in their commendation of 'rosy' and 'sparkling,' and in that fashion generalised drinks. They seldom give us the 'streaks of the tulip' as they should. So that a little preciseness may help, if only on a small scale and in a discursive fashion, to make the subject ripe and real to some extent, if not to the extent it deserves.

This notion of mine first took positive shape owing to the requests received from the editor of an enterprising, but alas, too short-lived period-ical, the *Piccadilly Review*. He actually published two of the chapters which should follow (the first and second). But the paper expired, with the third printed and the three next written in its dying grasp.[1]

I had from the first signified my intention of re-publishing, and Sir Frederick Macmillan had most kindly extended or modified (whichever be the proper word) his request for a big book to a provisional acceptance of this little one. So, recognising the clear risks, I set about it, with

[1] I have to thank the courtesy of its executors for restoring to me these fragments.

what result time may show. It is possible that someone, not a hopeless *bo*bolitionist, may say, 'Mr. Saintsbury appears to have spent a great deal of money on mere luxuries.' If I meet this 'by anticipation' (as some people say when they want to save themselves the trouble of a letter of thanks, having previously tormented others with one of request) it is not out of pusillanimity or a guilty conscience. But I would request readers to observe in the first place that the outlay here implied or acknowledged was spread over rather more than half a century; and secondly, that, as I have more fully explained in the little book itself, I very rarely bought more at a time than a single dozen of each wine named, nay, half a dozen or even odd bottles by way of experiment. In wine, as in books and other things, I have tried to be a (very minor) Ulysses, steering ever from the known to the unknown. Thirdly, for nearly twenty years of the time I was a journalist and in other ways a working man of letters—a state of life to which Thackeray's ejaculation, 'Grudge myself good wine? as soon grudge my horse corn,' doth more particularly and specially apply; while for full another twenty I occupied a position in which, as one received much hospitality, it was not merely a pleasure but a duty to show some. But I offer these as explanations, not excuses. There is no money, among that which I have spent since I began to earn my living, of the expenditure of which I am less ashamed, or which gave me better value in return, than the price of the liquids chronicled in this booklet. When they were good they pleased my senses, cheered my spirits, improved my moral and intellectual powers, besides enabling me to confer the same benefits on other people. And whether they were bad or good, the grapes that had yielded them were fruits of that Tree of Knowledge which, as theologians too commonly forget to expound, it became not merely lawful but incumbent on us to use, with discernment, when our First Mother had paid the price for it, and handed it on to us to pay for likewise.

As I have thus become almost wholly serious, there may be no great harm in continuing to be so for the rest of this preliminary canter. There was a time, not so very long ago, when one could afford to treat the adversaries of honest drinking with a good-natured and rather lazy contempt. They punished themselves, and they could not hurt us. But that time has passed. The constituencies have been flooded till they have become incalculable; the general commonsense of the country has been weakened by a washy overflow of so-called education; statesmen, never the most trustworthy of persons, have become utterly untrustworthy; and the great institutions which once were towers of refuge and strength against popular delusions have opened their gates to any rising of the waters. One was once pretty sure that whether a Bishop or a Judge was or was not personally a mirror of sanctity or a pattern of wisdom, mere silly and eccentric fads would find no favour with the one, and mere popular clamour receive no attention from the other. Everybody must decide for himself whether it is so now. But without venturing on any particular *scandalum magnatum*, it may be suspected that some people will entertain doubts on the point. Therefore it is well to keep the weather-eye open on this subject as on others, particularly because of one consideration. This is the extraordinary, though no doubt in many cases unconscious, *dishonesty* of the so-called Temperance party. All fanatics and all faddists are dishonest. A.M.D.G. is only the exaltation to a blasphemous superlative of their invariable and indeed constitutive habit of mind. But it is a question whether the most Jesuitical Jesuit of the most heated Protestant imagination has ever outdone a thorough-going temperance advocate in the endless dodgings and windings, suppressions and suggestions of his method. These phenomena are, of course, best studied, not in the extreme Prohibitionists, who have the honesty of Habakkuk Mucklewrath, but in the members of societies, which, professing to desire only restricted hours, limitation in strength of drink, heavy taxation, etc., are really working for prohibition itself by steps and degrees. Except 'Conscientious Objection' there was nothing more disgusting in the last five years than the duplicity of the cries, 'Oh! surely you won't drink *during* the war,' and 'Oh! you can't think of drinking *after* the war.' To guard against them it may be well for good drinkers to fortify themselves with the following facts, every one of which may be vouched for.

(1) There is absolutely no scientific proof, of a trustworthy kind, that moderate consumption of

sound alcoholic liquor does a healthy body any harm at all; while on the other hand there is the unbroken testimony of all history that alcoholic liquors have been used by the strongest, wisest, handsomest, and in every way best races of all times, and the personal experience of innumerable individuals in favour of the use. One of the most amazing audacities of these fanatics is the assertion that 'even moderate drinking shortens life.' A moment's thought will shew any clearheaded person that this cannot be proved without an exhaustive biological and clinical record of every moderate drinker since the beginning of time, unless there is a sophistic 'sometimes' slipped in, which renders the proposition practically valueless.[1] Stopping a horse in order to save someone else's life sometimes shortens the stopper's; and going to church on an inclement morning may do so. Moreover, that moderate drinking *always* shortens life, while it is insusceptible of proof, is, and must ever be, susceptible of *dis*proof. Everyone knows, or may know if he chooses, instances of moderate drinkers who have reached ages far beyond the average age of man, in a condition of bodily health which compares with that of most, and of intellectual fitness which should shame that of nearly all, teetotallers. One supposes that this monstrous inexactitude is founded on some kind of physiological experiment: and indeed, if you give, say,

[1] 'Quantification of the predicate' has been scoffed at. But in political logic it would often be valuable, and in the above instance it is a touchstone.

a mouse, even a small quantity of absinthe, or raw potato spirit, you probably may say that, 'moderate' drinking has shortened life. But otherwise the statement is one which no honest man should make, except as one of opinion, and no rational man credit, either as opinion or fact.

(2) The alleged costliness of these drinks is entirely due to legislation, and most of the money apparently given for them is really spent to carry on the system of the State, thereby relieving unpatriotic (and extremely ungrateful) teetotallers of their just quota. A bottle of whisky used to cost, at normal prices without duty, some few pence to produce; and a gallon of good small beer could at the same time be brewed *with tax* for fourpence.

(3) The argument about diversion of foodstuffs is equally, though in a different way, fallacious. Grapes certainly are food of a kind, but they are not a staple; the sugar used for brewing is not eatable sugar; wheat is practically never used for brewing or distilling; and, as has been shewn during a long period of sanity, of good work, and of good but not preposterous wages, there is no difficulty whatever in providing the whole world with plenty to eat and plenty to drink at the same time and at easy rates.

(4) As to abuse, *abusus non tollit usum* is the simple and sufficient reply to the fallacies drawn from that.[1] But one may go further than this and

---

[1] The supposed connexion with crime is reserved for the 'Conclusion.'

boldly say, with a certainty of saying the truth, that for every evil deed that fact or fancy or the unscrupulous exaggeration of partisans can charge on alcohol, it has prompted a hundred good and kind ones; that for every life it has destroyed or spoiled it has made thousands happy; that much of the best imaginative work of the world has been due to its influence; and that it has, as has been amply shewn of late, given 'more power to the elbow' of stout workers and fighters in the best of causes.

But we will not protest too much, and just finish this proem with something that does not in the least savour of apology. It is sometimes forgotten that only one of the two peaks of Parnassus was sacred to Apollo, the other belonging to Dionysus. The present writer has spent much of his life in doing his best, as he could not produce things worthy of Phœbus, to celebrate and expound them. It cannot be altogether unfitting that he should, before dropping the pen altogether, pay such literary respects as he may to the other sovereign of the 'duplicate horn.'

NOTE TO THIRD EDITION

THIS little book was reprinted with such un-expected rapidity that it was impossible for the author, without undue delay, to make a few corrections and add a little comment on its original reception. This reception was astonishingly and almost alarmingly favourable. I re-membered, like my half-namesake Borrow, a certain uncomfortable text of 'Woe'; and indeed the Fates did take some toll, unnecessary to specify, without long waiting. But the greediest author should have been satisfied and, if that were impossible, have had the edge of his appetite taken off by most of the reviews, not to speak of private acknowledgements. One disappointment, at least for a considerable time, I underwent. I had hoped for a little 'merry war,' as Mr. Kipling has it, with some champion of Pussyfoot. But such few blows as for a long time touched my pretty publicly exposed shield were curiously feeble, and even if meant to be dealt with the sharp end of the spear, obviously the work of clumsy instruments and prentice hands. The book, whatever its faults, certainly did not express or imply a desire (which one of the Pussyfoot *sbirri* imputed to me) to 'see guests under the table' at the close of the dinners it described: and the fact, suggested by the same or another as my test of an Earthly Paradise, that 'you could get blind drunk in Guernsey for sixpence' was only mentioned to emphasise the want of connection between serious crime (of which there was none there) and alcoholic cheapness. When, however, advocates are driven to this kind of advocacy, they are best left alone.

The encouragements I received were not limited to approval in reviews and letters—some of these latter from old friends of whom I had lost sight, and with whom wine, in its usual benevolent and beneficent fashion, thus reunited me. They sometimes took a very agreeably practical form. A gentleman of Liverpool, Mr. Holden, who represented the Spanish Produce Company of Cable Street, in that good city, wrote to me to ask if he might correct my ignorance (*v.*p. 110) of Spanish *cider* by sending me some. As in the other cases to be mentioned, I did not hesitate about accepting so good-natured an offer, and some very handsome bottles of 'Sidra Champagne' with a picture of a piper ('Gaitero') on the label duly arrived. They were not exactly 'Guipuzcoan,' like Burton's, but came from Villaviciosa in the Asturias (the 'Capital of the Filberts' of George Borrow himself), and so also represented

Northern Spain.[1] The liquor did not disappoint
the expectation raised by its receptacles. It was
rather of the Herefordshire than of the Devonshire type, but exceedingly well flavoured, of
good body, without being heady, and keeping the
balance between too sweet and too dry with great
success.

This, however, was not the end of my Nemesis-
provoking windfalls. Messrs. Hedges & Butler,
the well-known merchants of Regent Street, in
the same kindly and complimentary fashion,
informed me that they *did* possess some of the old
original Constantia (*v.* p. 69) bottled in 1862, and
requested my acceptance of a flask or two. My
own acquaintance with the wine was actually of
older date than that just mentioned, for it must
have been some years before my father's death in
1860: and anyone who understands the spirit of
this booklet will understand also the interested
impatience with which I waited till the gift could
be fairly tried. I wanted, naturally, to see what it
was like: but I wanted still more to see if I
remembered rightly what it *had* been like. No
disappointment came. I think—and its great age
in bottle would in any case make this likely—
that my recovered Constantia was a little paler in
colour and more delicate in body than her
ancestress of the fifties. But the flavour was 'true,'
and I had neither mistaken it earlier nor forgotten
it later. Charles Kingsley in *Hypatia* makes the

---

[1] If any one would like to know the makers' names, they were
Valle, Ballina y Fernandez.

naughty Prefect Orestes speak of Syrian wine as 'honey and fire.' The curious combination of honey- and grape-flavour in Constantia had remained in my memory, and if the fire did not now blaze or scorch, it glowed and warmed right well. Even with this, the genial pour of the gracious rain did not cease; for a representative of the great house of Sandeman[1] asked me to accept a brace of the most beautiful birds that ever fell to the longbow of a man of letters—two tappit-hens of that 1904 port of which I had only been able to praise the early development (pp. 29, 31). Ah! how I wished for the vessel described at p. 125, so that at last it might have accommodated its just quantum of nectar. But in the whole body of actual circumstances I could not have done either bird of Bacchus due honour at once; whereas when subjected to the process of decanting into flasks of less magnificent dimensions the wine came to my aid again and again.

So gentle and gracious are the compliments that pass between the folk of the meyny of the God!

If this document ever comes into use certain corrections of text will have been or have to be made. My chief blunder of fact was the remark (p. 28) that there was no evidence whether Barham

[1] As I have mentioned in the book, I have enjoyed more of Messrs. Sandemans' wine than of any other shipper's. As I have *not* mentioned, the three 'supernacular' ports of '70, '72, '73 (p.28) were, I believe, all of their shipping, and the only relic of my ancient cellar (stored in safe custody, I hope, but when to be drunk I know not) is a jeroboam of their '81, twice (see p. 23) rescued from dispersion.

was speaking of port or claret in his 3 + 10 years' prescription. It was a just penalty on me for not having taken sufficient care that my copy of *Ingoldsby*—a possession from boyhood and with early impressions of the illustrations—was excepted from the sale of my library and included in the salvage therefrom. He *does*, of course, mention port just before. I have accordingly made correction.

No other important mistake of fact occurs to me, though I have set right some minor slips of pen and press: but perhaps I should plead more or less guilty to some *paraphthegmata*, as the great rhetorician Aristides might have called them—'things I ought not to have said.' I have, I believe, wounded some worthy feelings in what I have written about White Port, and I *was* excessive: for it is not nasty, and is undoubtedly a good invalid's wine. But I never could see it without almost involuntarily and uncritically (and perhaps expletively) saying '*Why* [the something] aren't you *red*?' Several good persons, again, who have travelled have remonstrated with me on injustice to wines of Touraine and its neighbourhood. I ought to have said that I have never drunk them *in France*, thus giving them the direct (I intended an indirect) benefit of my remarks elsewhere on wines that perhaps do not travel well.

As to the more serious part of the booklet, the refusal or delay of any but negligible Pussyfoot reply prevents rejoinder. I will only mention one curious anecdote[1] buttressing my remarks on the

---

[1] Perhaps adding one *new* example of the amazing audacity of the

impudence of the 'moderate drinking shortens life' argument. A correspondent told me that some years ago there was a meeting of the governing body of Leicester Infirmary which was attended, among others, by no less than four governors over ninety, who outlived that age by years varying from 2 to 8, and not one of whom was an abstainer.

Perhaps one little concession to vanity may close this. A most well-wishing commentator seemed to be somewhat disturbed at the order of the wines in some of my *menus*, and to think that I had left it to the *chef* I mentioned. This was never the case; I should have brooked no such dictation either in regard to his own dishes or to my wines. The procession of the *dinner* wines is always deliberate. The *after*-dinner, as being set on the table together, may sometimes be more apparently—but not really—out of order.

But I will obey the rather peremptory question

---

scarcely camouflaged Pussyfoot. A few days before revising this 'Note' I saw, in a place already known to me as a good covert for this kind of fox, the statement that alcoholic drinks were 'fatal to a life of study.' It would be indecent to insist on any private reasons which I may have for amusement at this. I will merely remark that whosoever wrote it must, if honest, be utterly ignorant of the history of 'study' and students, in any and every branch of learning, science, scholarship or whatsoever name may be given to the exercise of the intellect. Unless, indeed, he was using the word 'fatal' in the rare sense of Dryden's charming 'Address to the Duchess of Ormond':

'For beauty still is *fatal* to the line.'

i.e.'fat*ed*.' But this would have been, in the more ordinary sense, fatal to his argument, not to mention that Pussyfoots and poetry are rarely acquaintances.

of King David and 'speak no more of my matters' or of other matters in this place. If I allowed myself to be tempted, as another kind critic suggested, to discuss such things as 'beeswing,' there were no end. But I may inform him that I once sought in vain for silk or samite of its colour to form part of a vesture for the lady of my house. I never could find an exactly satisfactory representative to qualify bodice, under-skirt and 'trimmings' for an overdress of silver-grey in a confection which I had imagined.

G. S.

BATH, *October* 23, 1920.

CHAPTER I

ORIGINS

THE late Mr. J. R. Planché, dramatist, anti-quary, Somerset Herald, and I believe excellent person generally, was not such a good poet as Dante or as Tennyson; and when he wrote, very late in life, in an address to Youth,

> 'I can do almost all that you can do,
> And I have what you have not, the Past,'

he might be thought to be blaspheming the doctrine of 'Nessun maggior dolore' and

> 'That a sorrow's crown of sorrow is remembering happier things.'

But after all he had Horace with 'Non tamen irritum,' and Dryden with his magnificent adaptation,

> 'For what has been, has been, and I have had
> my hour,'

on his side. At any rate, the other doctrine of 'make the best of it,' if base when applied to sublimer things, is grateful and comforting in the case of the lesser outrages of Fortune; and, if you have lost your cellar, there is still some satisfaction to be got out of your cellar-book.

The external aspect of this particular record, as it lies before its owner, is, like that of many other things of some internal preciousness, not imposing. It is merely an ordinary 'exercise book' cloth-backed, with mottled-paper sideboards outside, and unruled leaves within, undecked with the pompous printed page-headings for different bins and vintages, and the dispositions for entering consumption and keeping an eye on the butler, which the regular cellar-book boasts. It had been one, I think, of a batch, most of which were devoted to base purposes of lecture-notes, translations of ancient and modern authors, etc., etc. But it happened to be at hand and still blank when that owner first came into possession of a cellar, better deserving the name than the cupboards which do duty in most middle-class London houses; and so it was promoted. The actual entries in it cover, with some intervals due to domestic accidents, a period of exactly thirty-one years (the duration of some agricultural leases, I think), from 1884 to 1915. But the cellar, in the sense of the collection of wine which it represents, was some years older in formation than the record, and was founded in a great year for many things, wine itself included, the year 1878.

The foundation, I think I may say without vanity, or (since it has ceased to be) without undue provocation to Nemesis, took place under fair auspices, though it was then but a little one, extending only to a few dozen of various kinds besides ordinary claret. I started it with purchases from a certain excellent firm, then established on the north side of Pall Mall, who supplied my club, and with whom I had had a very few dealings before I came back to London. The managing partner was an old Scotsman, whose ideas were very sound and whose manners could be very agreeable. We discussed the firm's wine-list for some considerable time; and when I had made my scanty but careful selection, he accompanied me not merely to the door of his room but to that of the outer office. As we shook hands on the threshold he said to me, with the little bow which has almost disappeared:—'Mr. Saintsbury, Sir, if ye ask anyone to dinner and tell them where ye get your wine, we shall not be ashamed.' No doubt these things are, in two senses, vanity; but I confess that the wings of peace fluttered and flattered my soul as I walked past Marlborough House. Only, such speeches impose. I felt that I had a new duty on me; never to insult the pure society of these liquids by introducing unworthy companions to it. To say this is, of course, like publishing banns; it invites any unkind person to get up and say, 'You gave *me* bad wine.' But I trust I should find compurgators.

The cellar-book, as I have said, did not start for a few years after this, and when it did, most of the good wines which had earned me that compliment had done their good office. Only two, I think, survived. One was a Burgundy—Richebourg '69—of which my friend in Pall Mall had remarked: 'It ought to be good. The man we get it from sits up at night with a thermometer before it is bottled.' And, so far as I remember, that thermometer was justified of its information.

This wine was not more than nine years' old when I bought it; but Burgundy is quick in maturing. The other was of a far older vintage, and one of the three or four most remarkable juices of the grape, not merely that I ever possessed but that I ever tasted.

As to this point my merchant and mentor, despite his general approval of my judgment, and despite also the fact that the wine was the most expensive I bought from him, did not quite agree. 'Yes, it's great in its way; but it's a *coorse* wine,' he said. But I understood this as merely a piece of chivalrous partisanship, for he was (and no shame to him) a devotee of Bordeaux, and when he wanted anything heavier, of Port: and this was a red Hermitage of 1846. The Hermitage of the year before must have been made just before I was born; and I thought it very nice of the vines, whose ancestors are said to have been of Shiraz stock imported by the Crusaders, to have kept this produce till I was alive and ready for my first birthday present. For it was really a wonderful wine. When the last bottle of it was put on the table before I again broke up my household in London for a time, it was just forty years old. Now most red wines, if not all with the exception of Port, are either past their best, or have no best to come to, at that age. And with all respect to the

4

late Mr. George Meredith and some other persons of less distinction, I think that even those who have forty years' old Port in their cellars had much better drink it. But my Hermitage showed not the slightest mark or presage of enfeeblement. It was, no doubt (to translate, without 'betraying,' my friend's harsh epithet mildly), not a delicate wine; if you want delicacy you don't go to the Rhone or anywhere in France below Gascony. But it was the *manliest* French wine I ever drank; and age had softened and polished all that might have been rough in the manliness of its youth.

You had to be careful of it in some ways; one of the best-known of all my friends had very remarkable experiences as a consequence of neglecting my warnings, and consuming whisky instead of brandy with his soda after it. But there is no good in any man, woman or wine that will allow liberties to be taken with them. To champagne before it, it had no objection; nor, as hinted just now, to brandy afterwards. But it was uncompromisingly Gallic in its patriotism. They had only about a dozen and a half of it left in the wine merchant's cellars, and I bought the whole of it. But with a small supply like this and the certainty of nothing more like it (for it must be remembered that this was pre-oïdium and pre-phylloxera wine, and that the vineyards, by the time we drank it, had been ruined and replanted), it was rather a 'fearful joy' to take a bottle of it from the dwindling company. However, I was not in a position to give dinner parties every week, nor, to

5

speak frankly, did my company always deserve to have it set before them; so it lasted some years. It had, like all its congeners, a heavy sediment, and required very careful decanting; but when properly brought to table it was glorious. The shade of its colour was browner (people used, *vide* Thackeray, to call the red hocks 'brown') than most of the Hermitages I have seen; but the brown was flooded with such a sanguine as altogether transfigured it. The bouquet was rather like that of the less sweet wall-flower. And as to the flavour one might easily go into dithyrambs. Wine-slang talks of the 'finish' in such cases, but this was so full and so complicated that it never seemed to come to a finish. You could meditate on it; and it kept up with your meditations. The 'gunflint' which, though not so strong in the red as in the white wines of the district, is supposed to be always there, was not wanting; but it was not importunate and did not intrude too much on the special Hermitage touch, or on that general 'red wine' flavour which in some strange way is common to every vintage from Portugal to Hungary, vary as they may in character and merit otherwise. I do not say it was the best wine I ever had; that position I may be able to allot later.

Perhaps I may add something, though it may seem trivial or fantastic. I tried it with various glasses, for it is quite wonderful what whimsies wine has as to the receptacles in which it likes to be drunk. The large, slightly pinched-in 'dock-glass,' half filled, suited it as indeed it does almost

6

any wine. But whether it was mere whimsy on my own part or not, I always thought it went best in some that I got in the early seventies from Salviati's, before they became given to gaudiness and rococo. They were glasses of about the ordinary claret size, but flat-bottomed, and with nearly straight sides, curly-stemmed, with a white but rather cloudy body, an avanturine edge (very light) and deep blue knobs, small and sparsely set, in one row below it. They were good for all the great French red wines, but better for Burgundy than for Claret, and better for Hermitage or Côte Rotie than for Burgundy.

Alas!

The wine is gone, and with the wine went they, though many years after it. But of some other wines that they held and saw at the same time or later, we may talk further in other chapters.

Perhaps, however, a word or two on some matters connected with the above may not be offensive or superfluous. As may be supposed, I was not exactly a novice when I went to Pall Mall in 1878. I think I must have acquired some knowledge of good wine and an unlimited horror of bad from my father; for though he died when I was very young, and in his later years drank very little (chiefly, as I may again mention later, the modest Marsala, which used to suffice professional and city men of the mid-nineteenth century, and but a glass or two of that), I possess, among my few memories of him, a cellar-book of earlier date with quite respectable entries. When

I went to Oxford I joined no regular Wine Club for some private reasons, but used to give modest port and sherry 'wines' in my own rooms, *not* imitating one of my most distinguished and amiable instructors, who was said as a freshman to have produced two bottles, taken them up to the table, shaken them both, and then said, 'This is port and this is sherry; which will ye have?' One had one's share too of those feasts at certain more or less famous hostelries, where the bills used to run with a combination of detail and laconism: 'To share of dinner, sherry, hock, champagne, claret, port, brandy *and breakages—* £--s.-d.' I do not think I ever bought much wine in Oxford, remembering Dr. Portman's caution about 'the other shop,' and having dealings with an old friend of my father's in town. But I remember a good brown sherry of Guy & Gammon's.

From Oxford, after a brief interval at Manchester, with neither time nor means to invest in the gifts of Bacchus, I moved to Guernsey, where, as I have endeavoured to acknowledge elsewhere, things were as agreeable in this respect as in all others. Not only was liquor cheap, but it was *not* nasty.[1] I have mentioned some specialties in later chapters, and I will only add here that while my six years of sojourn there convinced me that

[1] Except some smuggled German potato spirit which an intelligent Customs officer, as he told us afterwards at whist, took from a newly planted cabbage bed. It was said to be all but absolute alcohol, and in taste 'more frightful than words can say,' as poets observe in their unimaginative moments.

plenty and cheapness of alcoholic liquor did not tempt to abuse of it, they also showed me that this same cheapness was a remarkable preservative of quality. The genuine article was so moderate in cost, and the possible profit on selling it was so limited, that adulteration was hardly at all tempting. Let me add that as the islanders included an unusually large proportion of persons of fair income, ancestral houses, and gentle blood, hospitality was abundant and the means of exercising it excellent. There can be no insult in recalling the fact that during the quarter-century of the great French wars the Channel Islands were the chief entrepôt of foreign-made drink— never mind whether in connection with what is called smuggling or not. Barely half a century more had passed when I went to Guernsey, and I do not think the last bottle of the old stocks had been drunk out.

But if Guernsey treated me well, Elgin, to which I went for some two years in 1874–6, treated me in this respect almost better; though of course one had to pay more for one's actual purchases. In that blameless Hyperborean district, what my predecessor at Edinburgh, Professor Masson, was soon after to call 'the savage observance of whisky toddy' (though this was only humorous irony like Lamb's on tobacco) lacked not observers. And the worship of the wine of the country did not exclude that of other cheerers. I never drank better claret or champagne than I had given to me 'up there'; and it was there that I began, on a very small scale and interrupted by the shortness of my stay, to form a sort of cellaret though not a cellar, and to study the subject as well as others in a manner worthy of it and of them. Alas! my first library and my first cellar had to be relinquished, as my last cellar and my last library were, in the same country of Scotland, forty years later. But it was in Elgin that I made my first separate study of a great English writer—Dryden; in Elgin that I began to read Elizabethan literature more than sporadically, and in Elgin that I laid the foundation of a real cellar, by selecting, not merely buying as offered, a 'classed' claret in the shape of '64 Ducru-Beaucaillou and a special champagne in that of '65 Krug.

My larger adventure there, like so many others, did not flourish (for reasons quite unconnected with the cellar), and vicissitudes followed, till, setting Chaucer at nought, I 'fled *to* the Press,' not from her, was most agreeably welcomed, and became in case to start a new collection of books and wines in the good year '78—the year of the second *Poems and Ballads*, and of the best Léoville Barton *I* ever drank (though Anthony Trollope thought '64 the *ne plus ultra* thereof); the year, finally, of which the Judicious Poet wrote to somebody or something unnamed:

> A year there was of glory,
>   Of promise false and fair,
> When Downing Street was Tory,
>   And England foiled the Bear;
> When all the wine succeeded
>   From Douro to Moselle,

And all the papers needed
   The wares I had to sell;
When, friends with love and leisure,
   Youth not yet left behind,
I worked or played at pleasure,
   Found god—and goddess—kind;
Played my last rubber cosy,
   Took my last miss at loo,
When all my world was rosy,
   But when I knew not—You!

And certainly though one did know the *Poems and Ballads* in the year itself, one did *not* yet know the Léoville. So perhaps the poem was written to *it*, and not to a lady-love, as might seem more likely to hasty observers.

CHAPTER II

SHERRY AND MADEIRA

THE first batch of these notes was, as it were
prefatory and promiscuous; it is time to be more
methodical. And that being so, no reasonable
person should quarrel if we begin with Sherry,
even as the truly good and wise usually do at
dinner.

It will be remembered that the Chevalier
Strong—speaking, it is true, to some extent
interestedly, but from wide experience and a good
taste and heart—warned Laura Pendennis on the
eve of her marriage, that there was nothing more
important to her husband's welfare than *pure*
'sherry.' And no doubt there was at that time, and
has been since, a great deal of sherry that no
honest and competent person could call 'pure.'
Although I am myself no lover of modernity, I do
not think there is, or was at any rate a short time
ago, quite so much bad sherry about as there used
to be. I remember in the middle of the sixties,
when Sunday lunching places in London were

rare and I had as yet no club, being driven to feed
with an Oxford friend at a small tavern or chop-
house in Piccadilly. The scorch and the twang of
what they miscalled 'Vino de Pasto' abide in my
palate's memory to this day. And it was and is all
the more wicked because Sherry is plenteous in
quantity and singularly various in kind.

I have always thought that Manzanilla[1] and
the other lightest growths and shipments of Xérès
and San Lucar and their neighbourhood receive
far too little practical attention in England. The
Spaniards, I am told, drink them in large, tall
beakers like our own old-fashioned beer-glasses
(curiously enough it is on record that Fletcher the
dramatist's 'maid had her sack in a beer-glass,'
but this was pretty certainly not Manzanilla);
and I can strongly recommend the practice.
Drunk thus, the wine provides a real beverage; it
goes with anything from oysters (with which
Chablis, though orthodox, does not please me,
while champagne, though it has Thackeray's
sanction, seems to me a sin without a solace) to
anything short of 'sweets.' Many of the other light
Spanish wines of this class (of the Riojas, etc., we
may speak separately) are excellent; for instance,
the lighter Paxarettes—that wine which most
literary people to-day associate only with Sir
Telegraph in 'Melincourt,' and of which it seems

---

[1] The Spanish traveller, Packe, quoted in Whymper's *Scrambles*,
attributes the peculiar flavour of Manzanilla to an admixture of
Artemisia nevadensis. This seems odd in the case of *wine*: but I may
have something to say on Artemisias in the chapter devoted to
liqueurs.

'dry' America sent us the other day a batch of butts. But some of the finer kinds are really supernacular—the best 'Tio Pepe,' for instance. Only, he who indulges in them must remember that they are an exception to the general rule that 'Sherry improves in the decanter.' When they are opened, the finer ones especially, they must be drunk. I have known a bottle of Tio Pepe become appreciably 'withered' between lunch and dinner.

Next to 'Uncle Joseph' in my book—indeed, as having occupied the same bin—I find entered a wine than which, except that both were sherry and both pale in colour, it would have been impossible to discover or even invent a greater contrast. The entry is, 'Pale Rich; Bot. 1865; Gee's sale, Torquay.' My friends the Messrs. Collier, of Plymouth, had bought it, and knowing that I liked good 'oddments,' handed it over to me. I think, but am not sure, that it was Wisdom's shipping. It *was* rich, very rich, almost a liqueur; but not in the least fulsome, and of a flavour which I never tasted in any other sherry. There is a well-known wine of the class called 'Nectar de Xérès,' some of which lay in the next bin in my cellar to this, but I always thought that the unnamed liquid deserved the title better; and an elect lady of my acquaintance (when ladies *do* know anything about wine, there is no mistake about their taste[1]) used to prefer it to any other that I could give her.

[1] In another case a hostess of mine (alas! now dead), tasting some Burgundy which her husband had put before us, looked at me and

One might jangle a long time on Montillas and Olorosos, Amorosos and the so vilely traduced Vino de Pasto itself; one might, perhaps, give a friendly hint to an ingenuous writer, such as those who think 'Carte d'Or' a special brand of champagne, that 'Solera' is not a particular *kind* of sherry. The Spanish wine merchants, or their English clients, have, moreover, a pretty taste for giving feminine names to this wine. My cellars (and even cupboards) have seldom for forty years been without a certain 'Margarita,' from some vaults in 'Bristol cit*ee*,' which were originally recommended to me by an actual Margaret, its namesake and fellow-citizen; and an 'Emilia,' an 'Isabel,' and a 'Maria' (more than one, indeed, for there is a *Tia* Maria, to match the Tio Pepe) have kept her company at various times without quarrel or jealousy. Even a 'Titania' appears in my book. But these are fantastries. Amontillado must not, perhaps, pass with such slight notice. The name has, of course, been far more widely taken in vain than that of Vino de Pasto, which is, after all, itself more general; and for the true, at least the perfect Amontillado flavour, you may

---

said, 'Isn't this corked?' Being less honest than Mr. Philip Firmin, I did *not* say anything rude, and equivocated. But she would have no 'transaction,' and as she went out of the room (she was small, and like all small ladies, especially when they are pretty, very firm in manner) she laid her hand upon her husband's shoulder and said, '——! you *must* send that bottle away and have another.' I can see at this moment, after many years, a great single diamond, which she used to wear slung on a loose gold chain, swinging forward and flashing as she bent to say it.

15

have to wait not a little time, while you certainly could not get it, even before the present 'dear years,' for a little money. Perhaps some people have forgotten, or never knew, how comparatively recent the taste for dry sherries is. It preceded, indeed, for a fairly long time that for dry champagne, but in both cases the 'dry'—alas! that the word should have acquired a new and blasphemous signification in the context!—is evidence of a general revolution in taste. It is, of course, true that people say 'sack' is 'secco,' and point to the old addition of sugar. But our ancestors of the sixteenth and seventeenth centuries had uncommonly 'sweet teeth.' We of the nineteenth century shed them, but the surprising fuss about sugar and jam recently looks as if they were coming back again.

The medium sherries—neither quite austere nor quite luscious—are, perhaps, more the wine of all occasions than anything else; and may be taken to utmost satisfaction with food or without it, at any time in the day, except the first thing in the morning and the last at night. But I own to an affection, mingled with regret, for the 'old golds' and the 'old browns' of yesterday, not to mention again such extraordinary things as the 'pale rich' already spoken of; and I own also that I think, though by no means accustomed to bewail things past more than reason, that they really have 'gone off.' Whether, in consequence of their diminishing popularity, less care is used in their preparation; whether there is some change in the natural wines themselves as there certainly has been in some others, I cannot say. But I can indicate with some precision the difference I perceive between the old 'East Indias' of fifty years ago and their representatives to-day. In those old wines the special flavour and the general 'richness' seemed to be thoroughly and inseparably blended; you knew that the wine was not 'natural,' but somehow or other it might have been. Nowadays, wines of ostensibly or nominally the same class, however old they may claim to be, and however much money you may pay for them, suggest a 'graft'—a stock of sherry with some particular character, and an inset of sweetening and flavouring superinduced. Which is a pity.

To finish with sherry, or at least the sherries on my list, let me note a wonderful Pedro Ximénès, stamped 'Sherry,' and furnished to me with the ticket 'very old in 1860,' by my constant friend in these ways, the late Mr. John Harvey, of Bristol, respecting whose cellars and those of his successors it may certainly be said:— 'There's *nothing* rotten in the *street* of Denmark.' It was not a wine for babes; but was curiously interesting to grown-ups in wine-lore.

It may seem irreverent to give so famous, and at its best so exquisite, a liquor as Madeira merely a postscript to the notice of its supplanter, which, by the way, it had itself supplanted. The proceeding is due neither to ignorance nor to contempt. For, in the first place, my father had many West Indian friends, and in early days I can remember actual apologies for giving one admir-

able Madeira—instead of contemptible 'Gladstone' claret. And, in the second, I know no wine of
its class that can beat Madeira when at its best;
the very finest Sherries of the luscious kind—even
'Bristol Milk' and 'Bristol Cream' themselves—
cannot touch it. But here, though by no means in
other matters, I can echo Swift's, 'Sir, I drink no
memories'; and I fear that the very best Madeira
is, and always has been since the pre-oïdium
wines were exhausted, mainly a memory. I had
some of these (both 'London Particular' in origin,
and from their special landing place in the West)
when my cellar-book started, but I seldom cared
to replace them with their degenerate successors,
and that for two reasons—First, the degeneracy
itself; and, secondly, the increased acidity. I
suppose Madeira always *was* acid: these southern
white wines generally are. Marsala certainly is,
and though the best sherry escapes, the old
practice of 'liming' sack (the object of which I
have known some people fail to understand)
speaks volumes. Now, I am sorry to say that I
have myself put into a glass of modern Madeira,
from most unimpeachable providers, a little
spoonful of carbonate of soda, with a result of
frothing that could hardly be surpassed by sour
beer. But let us not end on this uncheerful note.
Certainly a real old Bual or Sercial of the times
before 1850—I have drunk 1780 Madeira when
it was nearly ninety years old and in perfection—
was a thing to say grace for and remember. In
fact, I think Madeira and Burgundy carry com-
bined intensity and complexity of vinous delights

further than any other wines. There is possibly
something of the unlawful about their rapture,
something of the 'too much'—and accordingly
they are the goutiest of all juices of the grape,
whether pure or sophisticated.

The extraordinary *adaptableness* of sherry,
glanced at above, may deserve a few more words.
It does, perhaps, lend itself too freely to 'mixtures.' 'Sherry cobbler' is indeed a most excellent
drink. I was taught to make it when I was an
undergraduate by no less a person than the late
'Father' Stanton, who was as good a fellow as he
was a godly man; and the preliminary process of
'cataracting' the wine and the ice and the lemon
from two properly handled and not pusillani-
mously approximated soda-water tumblers is a
beautiful and noble occupation. But though my
adolescence almost coincided with the greatest
popularity of 'sherry and bitters,' I never cared
very much for that, and 'sherry and seltzer' has
always seemed to me a mistake. The lighter
sherries do not need dilution, and the heavier
appear to me to suffer a sort of 'break-up' of their
ethers in submitting to it. Since the scarcity and
monstrous price of whisky I have not infrequently
given sherry 'pegs' a fresh trial, but with little
satisfaction.

In fact the unusual range of alcoholic strength,
and the great diversity of flavour and body in the
different sherries make dilution almost unnecessary, except for persons who must have 'long
drinks.' As remarked above, Manzanilla will

carry you nearly through dinner, and others of the lighter class will go all through, though they may not be drinkable in quite such volume. I once even attempted a fully graded *menu* and wine-list with sherry only to fill the latter—a 'sherry dinner' to match the claret feasts often given by lovers of Gascon wine. It was before I began to keep such documents, and so I am not quite certain of the details. But if I were reconstructing such an entertainment now, and had the wherewithal as I once had, I should arrange it somewhat thus: Manzanilla with oysters; Montilla with soup and fish; an Amontillado with entrées and roast; an Amoroso or some such wine with sweets; and for after dinner, the oldest and brownest of 'old browns', say Brown Bristol Milk, which in its turn doubly suggests a finish to this notice. The very darkest sherry I ever possessed, indeed that I ever tasted or saw, was an 1870 wine specially yclept 'Caveza,' which I bought when it was more than twenty years old, and of which I still had some when it was over forty. It was not an absolutely first-class wine, but good enough, and remarkable for its extraordinary, and not easily describable colour—almost black except against the light. This brought about an incident slightly comic. I was giving a dinner-party in the early nineties, and a decanter of this wine was put on the table. Whereupon one of my guests (a medical man not quite so amply possessed of convivial amiability as some others of the faculty) proceeded positively to lose his temper over it. 'It was not sherry; it couldn't be sherry; there never was sherry of that colour; it must be queer-coloured port mislabelled.' Neither his host's assurances, nor those of his fellow guests, nor appeal to his own taste and smell would satisfy him; and things were getting almost unpleasant when I managed to turn the conversation.

CHAPTER III

PORT

THAT Port should follow Sherry is, or ought to be, to any decent Englishman, a thing requiring no argument. My cellar, if not exactly my cellar-book (which, as has been said, did not begin till some years later), was founded in this eminent respect on a small supply of 1851 (I think, but am not sure, Cockburn's), whereof my friend in Pall Mall, but from Scotland, who supplied it, ingenuously said that for his part he liked rich port, but that for a medium dry wine he did not think it could be surpassed. Nor have I, to my remembrance, ever drunk much better than this, or than some magnums of the same shippers and vintage which succeeded it, and were bought at the sale of that air-travelling victim, Mr. Powell, of Wiltshire. Indeed, I think '51 was the finest port, of what may be called the older vintages accessible to my generation, that I ever tasted; it was certainly the finest that I ever possessed. The much talked of 1820 I do not think that I ever drank *securus*, that is to say, under circumstances which assured its being genuine. Some '34, with such a guarantee, I have drunk, and more '47, the latter from when it was about in perfection (say, in 1870) to a date the other day when it was some sixty years old and little but a memory, or at least a suggestion. But '51 in all its phases, dry, rich and medium, was, I think, such a wine as deserved the famous and pious encomium (slightly altered) that the Almighty might no doubt have a caused a better wine to exist, but that he never did.

For some years, however, after the book was started I did not drink much port, being in the heat of my devotion to Claret or Burgundy after dinner. I cannot find that I ever possessed any '54, which, though not a large or very famous vintage, some not bad judges ranked with '51 itself, but I have records of '58, '61, of course '63, '68, '70, '72, '75 and '78 in the first division of my book, and before the interval in which I did not keep it regularly. During that interval I was accused and convicted of acute rheumatism, and sentenced, as usual, to give up port altogether—which was all the harder as I had just returned to my natural allegiance thereto. The result was that several dozens of what was going to be one of the best wines of the century, Dow's '78, comforted the sick and afflicted of a Cambridgeshire village; and that the only 'piece' of port that I ever laid down—a quarter-cask of Sandeman's '81—was taken back on very generous terms by the merchants who had supplied it. They gave me an additional five per cent per annum on what I had given for it.

However, other people had to be provided for, and I did not myself practise total abstinence. I seem, from menus preserved, though the book was in suspense, to have trusted chiefly to three kinds, no one of which perhaps would have been highly esteemed by a person who went by common opinion, but which had merits. One was a wine of uncertain vintage, believed to be '53, and probably Sandeman's, but certainly very good. Another was a Rebello Valente of '65. Now '65, like '53, has no *general* repute as a vintage, and some people think Rebello Valente 'coarse.' I can only say that this, for a 'black-strap' wine, was excellent, and I confess that I do not despise 'black-strap.' But the gem of the three was a '73 which had been allowed to remain in wood till it was eight or nine years old, and in bottle for about as much longer before I bought it. It had lost very little colour and not much body of the best kind; but if there ever was any devil in its soul that soul had thoroughly exorcised the intruder and replaced him with an angel. I had my headquarters at Reading at the time, and a member of my family was being attended by the late Mr. Oliver Maurice, one of the best-known practitioners between London and Bristol. He once appeared rather doubtful when I told him that I had given his patient port; so I made him taste this. He drank it as port should be drunk—a trial of the bouquet; a slow sip; a rather larger and slightly less slow one, and so on; but never a gulp;

and during the drinking his face exchanged its usual bluff and almost brusque aspect for the peculiar blandness—a blandness as of Beulah if not of Heaven itself—which good wine gives to worthy countenances. And when he set the glass down he said, softly but cordially, '*That* won't do her any harm.' But I am not entirely certain that in his heart of hearts he did not think it rather wasted on a lady, in which, as I have said, *I* think he was wrong.

I found out, at any rate, or chose to find out, that it did *me* none, or *si peu que rien*, and regretted my precipitancy in getting rid of the '78 and '81. But in ten years I had three house-moves and no good cellar; so that I simply used up what wines I had got and supplied deficiencies for immediate use only. When, in 1895, I settled in Edinburgh, it became possible and to me desirable, to make larger provision; and I set about it, though in a way perhaps not the most 'provident' in another sense. If you lay down a considerable quantity of an approved vintage port, just ready to bottle, you get it, or did get it, very cheaply. For nearly a hundred years before the war the price averaged some thirty to six-and-thirty shillings a dozen; it seldom or never plays the tricks that claret, in growing up, will sometimes do; it will treble its value in twenty or five-and-twenty years, and when it is matured, if you want to get rid of it, it will fetch full price. On the other hand, if you buy small lots of matured wines for your own amusement, you will pay a good deal for them, and broken dozens, or even larger lots sold at auctions will go for a song, while small lots of immature wines will go for whatever is worse than a 'song'. However, you have your amusement meanwhile, and must be prepared, as usual, to pay for it.

Between 1895 and 1915 I collected in this way small lots of most of the best back-vintages from '70 onward, with a few older still: and laid down a dozen or two of several sorts of the best that followed from '96 to '08 (I had bought but not cellared '11 before I gave up housekeeping). At one time I had, I think, about fifty or sixty different kinds of port, though seldom more than a dozen of each, sometimes only two or three bottles. The financial result when the cellar came to be sold was disastrous; but the amusement during the twenty years was great. You could continually try different vintages of one shipper, or different shippers of the same vintage, against each other; and as each year made a difference in the good wines, and these differences were never exactly proportionate, the permutations and combinations of experiment were practically in-finite, and always interesting in the trial, even if disappointing in the result. To find '70 and '73 always maintaining and improving their place to the very last bottle, when tears would have mingled with the wine but for spoiling it; to see the '90's catching up and beating the (as it seemed to me) always over-rated '87's: or to pit against each other two such vintages as '96 and '97 from the same shipper—these were intellectual as well as merely sensuous exercises, and pleasing as both.

One of the results of this extensive and continuous 'sampling' was the conclusion that the exclusive devotion of some wine-merchants to particular shippers is rather a mistake, and that the superior position accorded in the market to some of these shippers—Cockburn and Sandeman especially—is not universally justified. It is true that from the two shippers just named, and, perhaps, from one or two others, you will hardly ever get bad wine; but you do not get from them quite the same variety of good that you do from an enlarged range. I have done justice to Cockburn advisedly, and in the large number of Sandemans that I have had I have rarely been disappointed. But I don't think I ever drank—I certainly never had—a better '87 than some Smith Woodhouse; and I have seldom gone wrong with Graham, which I have heard experts (or supposed experts) patronise as 'very fair *second*-class.' There is no shipper's wine that I have found better than the best of Dow, '78 and '90 especially; Warre is almost always trustworthy; and Croft generally. Martinez and Offley, both famous names, have justified themselves with me, and so has Taylor, especially for somewhat rich wines. But the best rich that I ever had was, I think, a Cockburn of '81. Good wines I have had, in particular 'Zimbro,' of Feuerheerd's, but never, I think, the very best; and Kopke's famous 'Roriz' did not seemingly appeal to me, for I find none in the book.

On another point of great interest, the possession of so large a number of different vintages and shipments enables one to give a pretty well-based opinion; and that is the extreme uncertainty of the keeping qualities even of a fortified wine like port. I have already hinted, and may now state more precisely, my belief that no red wine will keep much more than fifty years without 'going off.' It is true that Barham was (as I had forgotten in the first edition of this book) speaking of port only when he wrote—

'And I question if keeping it does it much good,
After ten years in bottle, and three in the wood.'

But to claret this applies more strongly, though I think it applies to port, if not commonly, oftener than the general public supposes. The best and most robustly and skilfully prepared wines, such as '51, '63, '70, '73, '78, '81, '87, '90, and most '96's with some '97's, probably arrive at their best between twenty and thirty. But it is sometimes difficult to forsee how long they will keep at it. The most curious experience I had of this may finish the paper. Early in the year 1900 I bought from my Bristol friends some small parcels of the very best ports then available, including '70 (a really magnificent wine), and both '72 and '73. Comparatively few people may know of '72, but its price was then the same as that of the more famous '73, and for some time I thought it the better of the two, and got more of it; and this held for a year or two. But when the '72 had turned its thirty, the superior vitality of the younger wine began to tell, and in a few years more it was better than ever, while the more delicate 'Ventozello' of

'72 had certainly ceased improving and was even slightly senescent.

So no more, save a postscript, of 'the Englishman's wine'; though I should like to talk of a curious Dow, as deep in colour as a wine bottled at thirty months, but otherwise completely 'tawny' in character; of the '04's and their wonderfully rapid development (some which a friend gave me at Belfast, when it was not near Barham's limit, might have made a Sinn Feiner into a good citizen); of many other things. They are, to blend two lines of Mr. Swinburne's, 'past as the shadows on glasses'—the glasses in which they themselves were drunk; but the memory and the delectation of them remains.[1]

I subjoin a list of the ports in my cellar at different or the same times.

SHIPPERS AND YEARS

Cockburn	Dow	Croft	Sandeman
1851	1870	1875	1863
—81	—78	—85	—67
—84	—87	—87	—70

[1] One of the most agreeable incidents of my life in connection with Port is quite recent. Soon after I had published something about wine in the *Athenæum*, and since America 'went dry,' two students of that misguided country wrote to me saying that they had found it impossible to refrain, after reading the article, from sallying forth, purchasing some so-called port wine (I hope it was not very bad), and drinking my health in it. It would be difficult for a teacher to have a more gratifying testimonial to the efficacy of his teaching; especially when he remembers the boasts of Prohibitionists as to bringing on prohibition by sowing pseudo-scientific tarradiddles in U.S. school-books.

Cockburn	Dow	Croft	Sandeman
1890	1890	1894	1872
—96	—96	1900	—73
1900	—99	—04	—78
	1904		—81
			—87
Martinez	Warre	Graham	—90
1880	1878	1881	—91
—87	—84	—84	—92
1900	—87	—96	—97
	—90	—97	1900
	1900		—08

SHIPPERS AND YEARS

Silva & Cosens	Taylor	Smith Woodhouse	Feuerheerd
1887	1884	1887	1873
—90	—87	—96	—96
—96	—90	—97	—?
1901	1900		(bot. 1902)
—02			

Offley	Rebello Valente	Tuke Holdsworth
1887	1865	1890
—92	—90	

Gould Campbell	Burmester[1]	Uncertain
1892	1900	1853
1900		—58
		—61
		—68
		—70–74
		—73

[1] This wine, the only one of the shipper's that I ever bought, was sold before I tasted it.

(*Notes on Port List.*)

It should be observed that the relative frequency with which the names of shippers occur does not invariably involve a higher estimate on my own part, owing to the fact noticed in the chapter on the subject, of the partiality of some wine merchants for some shippers. This is especially the case with Sandeman and with Silva & Cosens, though I need hardly say that I find no fault with my advisers' taste in either case, especially in the first. And I have been informed, rightly or wrongly, that for some years past Dow's marks, which I think on the whole I have personally preferred to any others, have been in Messrs Silva's hands.

The wines of uncertain origin, it need also hardly be said, were bought merely on their merits. The '70, bot. '74, was a very curious wine, somewhat 'blackstrappy' and even 'public-housy' in character, but by no means to be contemned. Some of the later vintages, which I had in full bottle size, I never tasted, including one or two of the '96's and '97's, and I think all the 1900's and their successors. But the pints were 'morigerant' even up to the already-mentioned 1904, though mine was not quite so good as my friend's. Taking shippers and vintages all round, I should say '51, '58, '63, *some* '67, '70, '72, '73, '78, '81, '87, '90, were the best of those I drank in thorough condition. To make a still 'shorter leet,' as they say in Scotland, I think '51, '70 and '90 supplied the three best ports I have ever had. But though I don't exactly *envy* the people who bought my wine at prices which would scarcely buy Tarragona now—for Envy is not one of the heaviest of my quite heavy enough list of Deadly Sins, and I humbly hope for no long detention with wired-up eyes if I have the luck to reach the scene of that purgation—I think they made uncommonly good bargains.

For Port—*red* Port, as one of its earliest celebrants after the Methuen treaty no less justly than emphatically calls it, White Port being a mere albino—is incomparable when good. It is not a wine-of-all-work like Sherry—Mr. Pendennis was right when he declined to drink it *with* his dinner. It has not the almost feminine grace and charm of Claret; the transcendental qualities of Burgundy and Madeira; the immediate inspiration of Champagne; the rather unequal and sometimes palling attractions of Sauterne and Moselle and Hock. But it strengthens while it gladdens as no other wine can do; and there is something about it which must have been created in pre-established harmony with the best English character.[1]

---

[1] One thing it should not be asked to do, and that is to act purely as a thirst-quencher. I remember two stories illustrating this in a tragi-comic manner, though the tragedy predominated in the first, the comedy (with some romance) in the second. Mozley in his *Reminiscences*, I think, tells how a predecessor of his at Cholderton contracted a sad habit of excessive drinking. It appears that, in old days at Oriel, they used, as poor Hartley Coleridge found to his cost, to devise traps and torments for their probationer fellows (more recently I have heard of nothing worse at other colleges than expectation of salad-making). This man's trial was catalogu-

ing the library. It was in a state of dust not very creditable to the 'Noetics,' who had, however, hardly then arisen, and this dust had to be 'laid.' The youngster, perhaps too proud of his new status to drink beer, fled to port—then still the milk of donhood, as Greek was its unthreatened mother-tongue—and allowed the *Apeiron* to violate the law of the *Peras*. The other story is unpublished, and not so sad. A Canadian lady once told me that, when she was a girl, she was playing lawn-tennis with other maidens in the gardens of the late Professor Goldwin Smith 'over there.' It was a very hot day, and he came out and good-naturedly asked them if they would not like something to drink. (Goldwin Smith had a reputation for acerbity; but I can say that, on the only occasion when I met him—as being an old *Saturday Reviewer* he revisited his former haunts at the Albany, and my editor admitted me to the interview—he was as agreeable as any man could be.) Well, after a few minutes, during which the damsels naturally became thirstier than ever, their host reappeared, bearing on a mighty silver salver glasses of—port wine! They were not—or at least she was not—so ungracious as to refuse it; but it did not exactly meet their views.

CHAPTER IV

CLARET AND BURGUNDY

To write on these two glorious wines, giving them only some thousand words apiece, may seem audacious and profane, even with the limitation of the texts to the contents of a small cellar during a few years. But it has to be done; and the pleasure at least of doing it is not lessened by the fact, unpleasant in itself, that for a good many years past the writer has been unable to drink either. For his conscience is clear and his gratitude unmixed, inasmuch.as, for full forty years earlier, he never missed an opportunity of drinking his fair share of the best of both that came in his way.

I did not begin my cellar at a very good time (the latest seventies and early eighties) for Claret of the best class. The great '58's—respecting which Thackeray had enquired 'Boirai-je de ton vin, O comète?' and Fate had answered 'No'— were very dear, not very plentiful, and getting a trifle old. '64 was in perfection, but very dear likewise: and one was in danger of laying down those costly and most disappointing '70's, which, though they lasted in a rather unusual fashion and were drinkable at forty years old, were always more or less what wine-slang calls 'dumb.' Until the '74's and '75's were ready one had to pick up odd lots of crack vintages, and what one could of others which had turned up unexpected trumps. One of these latter, a '71 Lafite which hailed from Pall Mall, was a great stand-by; some '62 from the Powell sale, already mentioned, of the same premier wine, as it is vulgarly esteemed, a little less so. (For my own part I think the best Latour rather better, and a thoroughly 'succeeded' Margaux quite as good, while the outsider rival, Haut Brion —'Ho Bryen' as Pepys called it a quarter of a millennium ago — can be wonderful. I remember some Haut Brion of a friend's (it was '84), which for a short time — it did not, I think, 'hold' well — was at least the equal of any claret I ever drank.)

Of the 'regulars' of this period I see I had a beautiful Margaux of '58, and an almost equally beautiful Pichon-Longueville of '64, a Montrose (one of the least common of the second-growths in England, but charming at its best) of the same year, and another Margaux of '68. Of those unsatisfactory '70's I had at various times Lafite, Latour, Margaux, Haut Brion, Pichon-Longueville, Lagrange, and Croizet-Bages. The seven wines, taking only a dozen of each, cost, at the high prices then ruling for claret, about thirty pounds. I might have had three times the quantity of a sound *bourgeois* wine, much above

35

ordinaire, for the money, and no disappointment.

These things, however, will happen: and, especially on the 'small quantity, many kinds' principle, you get good compensation. I once bought some magnums of '75 Mouton Rothschild rather before it had established its reputation, at an extremely moderate price, and I need hardly tell anyone who knows claret-history what it turned out to be. I don't think I ever had a better: and it gave me one agreeable triumph. The late M. Beljame, one of the best of men, of scholars, and of foreign speakers of English, was dining with me. During dinner I had, perhaps rashly, said that I thought we got some of the best French wine in England, and he replied politely but doubtfully, 'Yes, you get some of the best, and,' with a little hesitation, 'some of the worst.' So I laughed and waited. When he had the Mouton in his glass I said, 'Now is *that* "from behind the fagots" or not?' And he bowed, as only a Frenchman can bow, and turned the phrase back into its native French with an emphatic 'Oui' before it.

As long as the '74's and '75's lasted nothing quite touched them; but I have always thought that the knowing ones seldom did justice to the '78's. It was customary to see and hear them described as 'coarse'; but they were certainly (to play a little on words) the last 'fine' wines for many years, if indeed there has been anything since equally deserving the epithet. With '78 *Château* Lafite I was indeed unlucky, for I bought, without sampling, several dozens of it when it was

36

eighteen or twenty years old, and found that it had evidently been kept in too hot a cellar. But I had some magnums of Léoville, already spoken of, and some others of Beychevelle of this year, than which I never drank any better representatives of those two admirable wines; and I also lit upon one of the 'bastard' Lafites, to borrow, without impoliteness, the term applied technically to lower class Montrachet—Lafite-Carruades—which had been originally bottled in or for Ireland, and which certainly justified the reputation of Irish claret. One very much preferred it to what used to be called 'Scotch claret'—a generous and potent but decidedly 'doctored' liquor, sold without name of vineyard, and suggesting a considerable admixture of the black wines of Cahors or thereabouts. This, however, had, I think, been practically obsolete for many years, even before the Caledonian deserted the purer kinds. After '78 there were catastrophes on catastrophes of mildew and the like, till you came to the strong, yet like the '70's rather hard and dumb, wines of '87, and the delightfully fresh and flavoury but rapidly withering '88's and '89's. But the last wines (for the '99's and '00's never seemed to me good for very much, and I have not tried later vintages owing to the causes mentioned) that I possessed and really rejoiced in were the '93's. The Latour of this year and the Rauzan Ségla, when eleven years old, were super-excellent; Montrose, Larose, Mouton Rothschild and Palmer were at the worst satisfactory; and I found something more than mere satisfaction in two outsiders—Gentiles, as it were, or at least trans-Jordanians to the pure Israel of Medoc—to wit, Pape Clément and Haut Brion Larrivet.

One thing may be noticed before turning away from a wine on which I could write a dozen or a score of these chapters, and that is the extra-ordinary drop in prices which this book of mine shows, and the cause of which people may assign at their choice to the falling off in the goodness of the liquor, or the falling off of the taste for it in Great Britain. As for the latter fact, I need only say that before I left Edinburgh,[1] the headquarters at one time of claret-drinkers, it was practically useless to open a magnum of claret for a dinner party of twelve or fourteen people, unless you selected your guests on purpose. And as for the price, taking the same growths at the same age of (1) the good vintages in the seventies, (2) the '93's, (3) the '99's and '00's, I should say that there was a drop of at least twenty-five per cent. between the first two, and a further drop of more than the same extent between (2) and (3). Even now, when all wine is at abnormal and pre-

[1] The first Lord Kinross, when he was Lord President, once told me that in his early days at the Scottish Bar it was customary for knots of four frequenters of the Parliament House, when a vintage promised well, to lay down as many hogsheads of the best reputed first or second growths, dividing the produce in bottles among themselves (a hogshead of claret makes about 23 dozen, so the subscribers would have that quantity apiece of the vintage, divided into lots of between 5 and 6 dozen of each growth). He added that he did not believe any of his brethren did any such thing at the time we were talking.

38

posterous prices, I see hardly anything, in the better classes of claret, quoted at figures parallel even to those which obtained thirty years ago.

If Claret is the queen of natural wines, Burgundy is the king: their places being taken in the other realm of the artificial by Madeira and Port. I was, during the keeping of this book, permitted by the kindness of my already mentioned friend, the late Mr. John Harvey, to be possessor of a small quantity of Romanée Conti '58. It was five-and-twenty years old when I bought it, and in absolute perfection; indeed, more than one good judge agreed with me that it was almost impossible to conceive anything more perfect in its kind. It is the fashion of course to put Clos-Vougeot at the head of all Burgundies, and very delicious Clos-Vougeot can be; but I never drank any specimen thereof equal to this for the combination of intensity and delicacy in bouquet and flavour, for body, colour and every good quality of wine. Indeed, Clos-Vougeot, excellent as it is, seems to me often, if not always, to have the excellences of claret rather than those of Burgundy; it does not 'hold to the blood of its clan' quite firmly enough. The '69 Richebourg which I mentioned in the first of these articles was also a fine wine, though it could not approach the Conti. The two were succeeded after some time (for one does not every day, unless one is both a millionaire and a Hercules, drink Burgundy of this class, though I cannot imagine a better *viaticum* in fetching Alcestis from the shades or any other difficult adventure) by others. The book was not kept in those times. But I find in *menus* of the date of the interval a Musigny of '77 and a La Tâche of '86, both of which I remember as delightful; as well as a Romanée of '87 which was good but which was a little injured, for me if not for others, by the memory of its great forerunner. Warnings of gout on my own part, and the annoyance of finding more and more people leave such treasures in the decanter, prevented my buying much Burgundy latterly. My last batch was a comparatively humble Corton of 1881, bought when it was nineteen years old for sixty-eight shillings a dozen, and quite cheap at its price. It lasted for at least a dozen years longer, and never went off at all.

But in earlier days the Richebourg was accompanied by a bevy of less distinguished representatives of the Slope of Gold and its neighbourhood—Corton again, Pommard, Santenay, Chenas and others—beverage wines which you paid some forty shillings a dozen or less for, and could drink without reproach of conscience, even by yourself. The bin was the occasion of a pleasant occurrence, which I may tell to the glory of my family, and perhaps for the amusement of the reader. One of my father's sisters was a very old lady, who lived by herself in a remote part of the country on no large income, and (as the phrase goes) in a very quiet way. Having some trouble with her eyes, she came up to town to consult an oculist, and naturally stayed with me. The oculist, finding nothing organically wrong, but only a certain weakness of age and constitution, recommended her to drink Burgundy. I gave her on successive days some of the Richebourg, telling her frankly that it was a very expensive wine, and some of a sound Pommard, which could be had for between half and a third of the price, that she might choose and order some from the merchant, who, as it happened, supplied both. I had imagined that the first figure would either frighten or shock her; but she said with perfect simplicity, 'I think, my dear boy, the best always *is* the best,' and ordered a small supply of the Richebourg forthwith.

One more Burgundy story, perhaps, to finish with. A vast number of years ago a friend of mine, who had some offical business with one of the great rose-growers in the neighbourhood of London, asked me if I should like to go with him. We went down by train, and after the business was done and the gardens thoroughly surveyed, were entertained with a most copious and capital lunch, or rather early dinner. To vary a poem which Mr. Gladstone once adapted to rally his great rival and 'the farmers of Aylesbury,' 'with the salmon there was sherry, with the mutton there was beer'—some of the best draught Bass that I remember. But when we had done justice to it all, our host produced a bottle of very special Burgundy—Chambertin,[1] I think—which had

---

[1] It may have been noticed that I do not mention any of this famous wine as in my own possession. The fact is that it has never been a favourite of mine. It may be blasphemous to call it 'coarse,' but it seems to me that it 'doth something grow to' coarseness, as

been given to him by a correspondent at Dijon itself. It would never have done to refuse it; nor perhaps (for we were both young men) had we much inclination to do so. So we submitted to 'the sweet compulsion' and took our leave. But then came the question, 'What to do next?' It was a warm summer afternoon; and, though England produces nothing better than beer and France nothing better than Burgundy, it is difficult to imagine two beverages which agree worse together. Had we taken the train again we should probably have fallen asleep, and been waked ignominiously and in a flustered condition by the ticket-collector. So we made up our minds to walk the ten or twelve miles, and did it. I remember that for the first part of the way I felt as if there was a thin India-rubber or air-cushion beneath the soles of my boots. But there is hardly anything that you can't 'walk off,' and we walked off this pleasing but perilous predicament.

(*List of 'Classed' and other clarets in cellar at various times. The 'outside' vineyards are italicised.*)

1858—Ch.	Margaux
1862— ,,	Lafite
1864— ,,	Pichon-Longueville
,,	Montrose
1868— ,,	Margaux
,,	Dauzac
1869— ,,	de Beychevelle
,,	Kirwan

compared with those preferred above. It was Napoleon's favourite; and the fact rather 'speaks' its qualities, good and not so good.

1870—Ch. Lafite
   ,, Latour
   ,, *Haut Brion*
   ,, Margaux
   ,, Pichon-Longueville
   ,, Lagrange
   ,, Croizet-Bages
1871— ,, Lafite
1874— ,, Léoville-Barton
   ,, Rauzan
   ,, Palmer
   ,, Giscours
   ,, Branaire-Ducru
1875— ,, Mouton-Rothschild
   ,, Durfort
   ,, Duhart-Milon
1878— ,, Lafite
   ,, Latour
   ,, Léoville-Barton ⎫ *Magnums, and*
   ,, de Beychevelle ⎬ *both quite*
           admirable
   ,, Langoa
   ,, Dauzac
   ,, *Lafite Carruades*
1883— ,, Margaux (*magnums*)
1884— ,, Durfort
1887— ,, Lafite
   ,, Cos d'Estournel
   ,, de Beychevelle
1888 ⎫   D'Issan, La Lagune, Beychevelle,
   ⎬ ,, Clerc-Milon, *Smith Haut Lafite*
1889 ⎭
1891— ,, Mouton d'Armailhac
1892— ,, Duhart-Milon
1893— ,, Latour
   ,, Rauzan-Ségla
   ,, Montrose
   ,, Gruaud-Larose
   ,, Mouton Rothschild
   ,, Palmer

43

1893—Ch.	de Beychevelle
,,	*Pape-Clément*
,,	*Haut Brion Larrivet*
1895— ,,	Palmer
1896— ,,	Léoville-Poyferré
1899— ,,	Margaux
,,	Mouton Rothschild
,,	Pichon-Longueville
,,	Gruaud-Larose-Sarget
,,	Léoville-Lascases
,,	Cos d'Estournel
1899— ,,	Langoa
,,	Calon Ségur
1900— ,,	Margaux
,,	Léoville
,,	Langoa
,,	Pontet-Canet
,,	*Pape-Clément*

(*Notes on Claret List.*)

Some additional notes on a few of these may be interesting. The magnums of Margaux 1883 may surprise connoisseurs, for the year had a very bad reputation, mildew having attacked the vines. I saw them in an auction-list years later, and, having made a bid for a few, was offered the whole lot —several dozen —at an absurdly moderate price, 3s. 6d. to 4s. per magnum. They were actually *premier vin*, château-bottled and in quite good condition, though the wine was light in body and not very full in flavour. I drank them, while they lasted, in place of ordinary Medoc of about the same price, and a very good bargain they were. About the same time or a little later, when I

44

was not keeping my cellar-book regularly, a bottle or two of, I think, Langoa, dating from the mildew years, developed an extraordinary malady, arising from the presence of what I believe the chemists call caproic acid. The stuff tasted and smelt abominably *hircine*.

The wines italicised above are, of course, inhabitants of the Court of the Gentiles— outsiders as regards the offical list—though Lafite *Carruades* is, I believe, actually a neighbour of the greater vineyard. Haut Brion *tout court* every one who knows anything about claret is acquainted with, and it is spoken of above. Haut Brion *Larrivet* is not much below the chief of the clan. Another Gentile, Smith Haut Lafite, was un- noticed among the examples of those two curious years, '88 and '89. They 'came up as a flower' and faded like one—but for freshness and passing pleasure of flavour and bouquet—for drinking at a draught—they were charming. Browning's 'A Pretty Woman' is the poem that reminds me most of them.

Some readers may be surprised at seeing Pontet Canet figure only once in the list, and that only among the 1900's. It became, in the odd way in which things do so become, a 'literary' wine a good many years ago; but I never cared for it. Almost all the wines of its own (Fifth) class that I know seem to me as good or better—Batailley, Dauzac and Mouton d'Armailhac decidedly bet- ter. Of other classed wines which do not figure at all in the above list, but which I have possessed or at least drunk at different times in my life, Brane-

Cantenac and Ducru-Beaucaillou have left best memories among the second growths; Malescot Saint-Exupéry among the third; Branaire-Ducru and Le Prieuré among the fourth. Of all the elect—between 50 and 60—only some half score are quite unknown to me, and these include, I think, no seconds; only Ferrière and Marquis d'Alesme among the thirds; but Saint-Pierre, Talbot, Pouget, Marquis de Terme and Rochet among the fourths; and Grand-Puy, Pedesclaux, Belgrave and Camensac among the fifths. And I should not have left them untried if I had ever seen them in any wine-merchant's list during the time when I could drink claret.

I have said nothing about the wines of Saint-Emilion—even the noted 'Cheval Blanc'— because I have never cared much for them. But I certainly do not wish to say anything against them. And to mention all the good non-classed wines, Medoc or not, that I have drunk and enjoyed would be endless. In the days above mentioned—the Time of Roses—I have had divers half-hogsheads of such wines bottled in half-litres or Imperial pints for ordinary drinking, and thanked the Lord therefor. Some such wines—for instance, a good *premier bourgeois* Margaux—will turn out just as well as any but the best classed growths, and might be drunk 'before the dear years' with no sense of extravagance. Perhaps no wine's name has been more taken in vain in England than Saint Julien's. He must be a fortunate claret-lover who has not sometimes made grimaces over a bottle so labelled[1] at the average British hostelry. Exactly why this poor district has been so abused I do not know. It is true that some of the very best vineyards (Léoville, Larose, Ducru-Beaucaillou, Lagrange, Langoa, Beychevelle) are situated there. But Margaux (one of the silliest examples of 'facetious and rejoicing ignorance' about wine that I remember was a jibe at the difference of Margaux and Château Margaux) and Pauillac (which actually has two of the three first growths, Lafite and Latour, with the scarcely inferior Mouton Rothschild and Pichon-Longueville to back them up, and not a few excellent fourths and fifths) have very much fewer tricks played on them, and others, except Saint-Estèphe, hardly any at all. Perhaps relative abundance of produce gives the reason.

I have endeavoured to keep clear of the most commonplace topics in these notes. Perhaps, however, something should be said on two such. I have lived through two or three different phases of attitude to the temperature at which claret should be drunk. There was the Ice Age—certainly a barbarous time. It is well that Browning's 'Bishop Blougram' was not an Anglican prelate, for his directions to my sometime colleague in journalism, Mr. Gigadibs,

> Try the cooler jug,
> Put back the other, but don't jog the ice,

---

[1] There is one label in particular which is very common, and which I learned long ago to shun. But the peculiarities of the law of libel prevent my specifying it.

are very harrowing. Icing good claret at all is, as has been said, barbarous; but the idea of subjecting it to processes of alternate freezing, thawing and freezing again is simply Bolshevist. Some readers may remember 'marsupial' claret jugs with a pouch for ice. Then came the warming period, determined by not always well understood imitation of French ways. (It is in one of Sandeau's books, I think, that an uninvited guest complains of the claret being unwarmed and the champagne un-iced.) Unfortunately, people used to put it close to the fire and parboil it. Now, and for some time, the books have recommended nothing more than bringing it up in time to let it get the temperature of the dining-room, which is sound enough. As for Burgundy baskets, they are pretty instruments, and may be useful—when the cork is not first drawn with the bottle perpendicular. But to make them of any real good, the *whole* of the contents should be poured into successive glasses, at only the necessary inclination, till the sediment is reached, and no tilting back permitted.

CHAPTER V

CHAMPAGNE AND OTHER FRENCH WHITE WINES

Who was the author of the celebrated, or once celebrated description, 'A man who likes [or 'who would say he likes'] dry champagne'? It indicates a period so far back that only the oldest of us remember it. It is true that you may find the offer of 'champagne, sweet or dry' in books of still earlier date, but the 'dry' there was, I believe, *still* dry Sillery. However, the change came: and it was not finally accomplished when my cellar-book was started. The head of the great house of Roederer was, even later, said to have declared that as long as *he* lived there should be no bowing to the dry Baal in his cellars; and, at any rate in the country, Clicquot was more often still sweet — not to the 'Russe' extent, which was only good for savages or children, but yet not dry. Indeed I remember how, when I confessed to my Pall Mall mentor in the opening interview, that I did not share the prevailing mania for Pommery, he looked at me approvingly and said, '*I*'d nearly as soon have a bra-a-andy and sod-d-a!' Nevertheless if you only keep sufficient wine-flavour in dry wines (they are apt to lose it) nobody of catholic taste would desire their abolition, though one may regret the moderately rich and full-flavoured variety as an alternative.[1] And as a matter of fact, the earliest pages of my book show Pommery itself and Heidsieck Monopole, Perrier Jouet's 'Club Dry' and even Dagonet's 'Brut Exceptionnel.' This last used to be (I think it has gone off lately) a considerable favourite with me, though I have heard some people say they would rather drink camomile or calumba. And, taking well-known brands all round, I do not know that I was more faithful to any than to Krug. I began my fancy for it with a '65, which memory represents as being, though dry, that '*winy* wine,' as Thackeray describes it, which Champagne ought to be, but too seldom is. And when, just fifty years after that vintage, I drank farewell to my cellar before giving up housekeeping, it was in a bottle of Krug's Private Cuvée, 1906.

Still, I had no monomania on the subject. I think there were few of the greater brands that were not represented by a modest dozen or two at

---

[1] The optimists who hold that there is in all evil good may point to the effect of U.S. 'dryness' in acquainting *us* with 'Goût Américain' champagne. It seems to me (I am sorry to shock Mr. Walter Leaf, both as a scholar and as a colleague in scholarship of two intimate, though alas! now dead, friends of mine; but at least I did *not* give '30os. a dozen' for my specimen bottle) a not unhappy compromise between asperity and mawkishness.

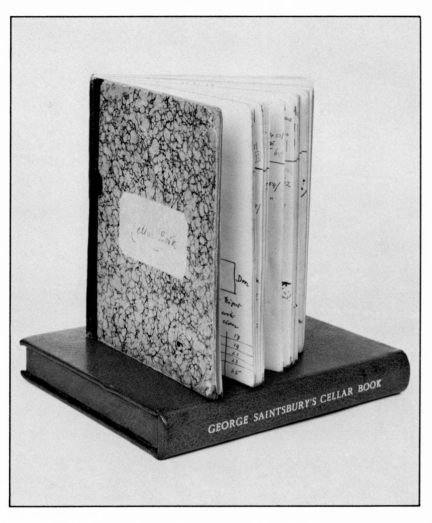

The original cellar-book, an 'ordinary exercise book, cloth-backed with mottled sideboards outside, and unruled leaves within', and the handsome leather-bound volume that fetched £1,550 in 1977.

On the following pages are some leaves from the book, in the Professor's own hand.

Plan of Cellar

Window

L   R

Door

Bins on left
as seen with back
to door

1	2	3
4	5	6
7	8	9
10	11	12
13	14	15

Bins on right
as seen with
face to door

16	17
18	19
20	21
22	23
24	25

top back of all. 6.2.02
2 doz. rows 99 bot. 18/ (.S. 30/)
from all 1 " Cockburns 96 bot. 98? " 38/
(bot 84) sealed bottles

— Jerboams #1 Port (Harvey)
20.3.02 Easter Eve 1 doz. 96 6-8/ World row 34/
1 " " " Graham 38/
(permanently put up after a to row row ?all
a cellar at Plymouth (posib for)
Cellar 9.9.01 nov. 98
2 mags. coll. real pints 96 Port bot 98 R.
Cockburns blah. Sel. 4 (cockburns 20/
Fenwick: 4 2 Jumbo
B.M. R.J.

2 doz (wfts Port +885 8

Kumpound
10 of 55/ (.S.S.A)
more a shop

8.1.01.
(cleart Newton Milton 92) Moculder
from a
" Palmer 95 1 doz. adala (R.K. 30/
96
15.3.01 " Beych ville 1 doz (Pfordan 28/)
(Below) Leoville Poyferré 96 (" 38/)
cross his by drawing room.

(Claret

1904 *Grand Larose* 1.0
Langoa Barton 1.0

1870 Marquise Pichon Lon-
gueville & Lagrange 2.3

1878 Lafite 3.0
(do old barel) 1
Léoville (St maps) 10
Feb 02 Lafite (overg falles) 2.-
Beychevelle (" ") 10
Oct 01 1887 Léoville Browner 3.
1888 Lafite
1889 } many ou Bin sowt 2.6
1891 } moulin a Communilhac
1892 Duhart Milon 1.-
+1.-
1893 au op.
1895 Palmer 1.-
1896 Beychevelle 1.-
Léoville Poiferré 1.-
1899 au op. { Marquise Léoville 6.
1900 au from Bars { Larose Barton Claret 4 5

one time or other in my cellar; and the very best I ever had was a Perrier-Jouet, obtained through the same kindness which supplied me with the Romanée Conti already mentioned. It was a wine of the great vintage of 1857, and was supposed to have formed part of a parcel originally shipped for Queen Victoria, and designated 't.c.' that is to say *très coloré*. When I bought it, May 1884, it was twenty-seven years old, of a deep amber colour, and nearly but not quite still, though not at all ullaged (alas! there are some people who do not know that ullaging sometimes improves champagne. But they, as the Colonel said to the Cornet who did not know that age improved it, 'have a great deal to learn'). It was so majestical that one was inclined to leave it quite alone, and drink it like a slightly sparkling liqueur. But I was tempted—not I think exactly or wholly by the devil—to try if the immense dormant qualities of it could be waked up. At that moment I also had some '74 of the same shippers, than which there can have been few better—just in perfection, ten years old, all rawness gone, but sparkle in fullest force. So I married them, and the voice that breathed o'er Eden did not refuse to repeat itself, *mutatis decenter mutandis*.

'The bigger the better' is, though a common, not a universal rule; it does not, for instance, apply to fish, nor to mutton, nor to some other things edible and not edible. But it generally applies to receptacles of wine, and to those of champagne very specially. Jeroboams, or to be accurate, double magnums, to which the term

51

Jeroboam, properly applying to a *six* bottle vessel,
is often by courtesy vouchsafed, are costly and
risky, for a corked one is no joke of a loss. They
require a properly adjusted company to drink
them, and an intelligent Ganymede or Hebe (I
have known Hebe do it beautifully) to pour them
out. But you never get such good wine as in or
from them. As for vintages, I thought the '70's
(with which, in the way of laying down, I started)
very good indeed, but Champagne vintages are
perhaps better known than any others, so that
there may be no need to waste time on them.
Sometimes there were interesting conflicts of
adjoining years, especially in '92 and '93, and
later in '98, '99 and 1900. The knowing ones
usually went for '92, which was, if I remember
rightly, the smaller and selecter vintage. I had
some good wines of it—Pommery and Krug and
Roederer among them. But the vintage that I laid
down most of, and liked, I think, almost best of
all, was '93. It took, in some cases, a long time to
develop; the Clicquot, at eight and even nine
years old, had a peculiar bitterness. But this
worked itself out; it became a very perfect wine;
and though its seventeenth winter was certainly
not 'sweet,' as seventeen is supposed to be, it then
had all other excellences that such a wine ought to
have, and retained them till over twenty. Nor
were the others, as each came to perfection, much
behind it. I find special notes of admiration on
Moët, Ayala, and St. Marceaux—the last a
shipper rather undervalued, I think, south of
Tweed, though respected duly north of it. As for

the three competitors of the end of the century, I should select Clicquot '99 as the best of a dozen good ones.

But champagne is—or was[1]—everybody's wine, and needs little talking. Nothing, perhaps, does you so much good if you do not drink it too often; but, for my own part, *'toujours champagne'* would nauseate me in a week or less. One thing, as a pendant to what was said on the price of claret, may be added: and that is, that as Bordeaux put its prices down Reims sent them up. In the late seventies one was seldom asked more than ninety shillings for the very best vintages, ready to drink, at eight or nine years old. Five-and-twenty years later ninety-five and a hundred were demanded for wine just sent over, and wanting years to fit it for drinking.

Perhaps, too, I should here say something, as in the Claret chapter, on the question of temperature. Ladling bits of raw ice into a glass of champagne at dinner is no doubt again barbarous; though hosts who have given their guests doubtful wine may be glad to see it done. Nor do I myself approve of the ice-pail; for extreme cold certainly hurts flavour. But there is no doubt that most people *do* like their champagne cold; indeed, even on some bottles of white Bordeaux, you may find directions to 'ice.' It is also certain that cold assists the 'pick-me-up' character of sparkling wine. Matthew Arnold, in one of his letters, notes how 'the cool champagne at dinner' relieved a

---

[1] I don't think I have drunk it a dozen times in the last three years, or thrice in the last twelve months.

previous touch of the heart-weakness, which was in the end to prove fatal to him. For my own part, I have always found that, except in extremely hot and close weather, wrapping the bottles in a cloth wetted with water fresh from the tap (or better still, a well), and placing them in a draught for a short time, gives all the coolness necessary, and does not 'numb the ethers.'

It is, perhaps, too bold to attempt to deal with the three great groups of white Bordeaux, Burgundy and Hermitage, those of the Loire district, and the innumerable *petits vins blancs* of the rest of France, in the tail of a chapter. But the restriction of these papers to a single small collection makes it less impudent. The last-named group are almost unobtainable in England, and, indeed, might not travel. I never cared much for the wines of Anjou, Touraine and their vicinage, either sparkling or still. Medical favour has for the last two or three decades greatly popularised Graves and Barsac, but it has always seemed to me that no wines lose more by crossing the channel. On the other hand, the fuller Sauternes travel very well, and in their way are noble.

I say 'in their way,' because there is a curious difference between white and red wines, as it seems to me. The last glass of your bottle of good Claret or Burgundy (I mean of the bottle when you drink the whole) is as good as the first. I am not sure that it is not better. But the first glass of the corresponding white wines—be they Château Yquem or Montrachet themselves—is a great deal better than the last; indeed, this last has a tendency to 'sicken,' as is also the case with white Hermitage, and with the heavier hocks. At least, that is my experience; and I have found many, though not all, good drinkers disposed to agree with me.

Still, all these wines, when good, are very good gifts indeed, and if you find that too many glasses spoil their effect, the obvious remedy is to drink fewer. I should, indeed, never drink them—with the possible exception of white Hermitage—*after* dinner; and the fact that Thackeray did so once— at somebody else's suggestion, it is true—seems to me almost the only blot on his wine-record. But the lighter—not *too* light—kinds, such as good Carbonnieux or Olivier of the western branch, or a good Pouilly of the eastern, are admirable dinner wines. And, *in themselves*, such wines of the greater clans, as Châteaux Yquem, Coutet or Latour Blanche, as Montrachet, and even a very good Meursault ('70 of this was first-rate),[1] all of which made their home with me at different times, are always memorable. With an unnamed Haut Sauterne of '74, bottled by one of the oldest Edinburgh merchants, but bought at somebody's sale, I have specially fond associations. It was a very rich wine, being about thirty years old when I first had it; in fact, it was too rich for some tastes. But once there came to 'the grey metropolis' a Finnish lady—a most perfect representative of

[1] The same lady who praised my 'Pale Rich' Sherry (*v.* Chap. II.) was good enough to remember most *donnescamente* (as Dante says) this Meursault, many years afterwards.

NOTES ON A CELLAR-BOOK

non-Aryan beauty and anythingarian charm—
to whom not only all men, but what is more
wonderful, most women, fell captive the moment
they saw her. She was dining with us once, and
confided to me, with rather a piteous *moue*, that,
in this country, champagne was 'so dreadfully
dry.' Fortunately I had remembered beforehand
that the warlocks and witches of the North like
sweet things; and had provided a bottle of this
very Sauterne, of which I had a few left. She
purred over it like one of Freya's own cats (let it be
observed that I do *not* think Freya was a Finnish
goddess), and I promised her that I would keep
the rest for her. But alas! she left Edinburgh in a
short time, and after no long one I heard that she
was dead. The wine lost half its flavour.

Sparkling white Burgundy can be very good,[1]
the best of all the imitations of Champagne. I
have spoken of the lighter still wines. As for
Montrachet,[2] it is very great, though, as someone

---

[1] Some which we used to get in Guernsey *before* the war of 1870
(the supply stopped then) was the cheapest *good* sparkling wine I
ever had. It cost, unless my memory plays tricks, but thirty
shillings a dozen, certainly not more than thirty-six shillings; and
the shop where I bought it—a queer emporium of furniture,
curiosities, second-hand books and Heaven knows what else—was
the only place where I ever heard Victor Hugo speak. For
sparkling *red* Burgundy I have never cared; nor indeed for any red
'fizz.' 'Old Rose' champagne was sometimes delicious, but it was
not *red*; and its modern deeply 'pinkified' representatives please
me not much. The true *œil-de-perdrix* tint is not, I think,
'synthetically' attainable. But a perfect 'partridge-eye' champagne might almost deserve, on the pattern of 'pheasant-eye'
narcissus, the epithet 'poetic.'
[2] This magnificent and formidable wine has three degrees or
qualities, *Aîné, Chevalier* and *Bâtard*. The last is not the least

56

says, I think in Freytag's best novel, it 'makes one's veins swell like whipcord.' With white Hermitage I have twice been lucky—once with a lighter wine, Château Grillet or Grillé, which used to be a favourite here in the days of the Regency, and once with a heavier, La Frette. This last was one of the ornaments of my cellar. It was a '65, and was nearly thirty years old when I bought it at a sale in Edinburgh, but before I went to live there, a friend taking some of the batch off my hands. It was not 'done for' twenty years later still, when it had reached its full half-century; but it wanted re-corking, and the 'gun-flint' taste had grown too strong for most people. At its very best, it was unique—a worthy sister to its twenty years elder, and at this time departed, *red* brother, celebrated in Chapter I.

---

noteworthy of the denizens of Sinister Street; the Chevalier I do not think I ever drank; but the 'eldest' certainly deserves his pride of place.

CHAPTER VI

HOCK, MOSELLE AND THE REST

GERMAN wine has of late naturally shared the unpopularity of German everything—naturally, but not wisely. The true attitude in such matters was long ago put in the 'War Song of Dinas Vawr':

> His wine and beasts [*provide*] our feasts,
> And his overthrow our chorus.

Not that Hock, as indeed was hinted in a former chapter, has ever ranked with me among the 'First Three,' or even the first five or six greatest wines. The 'palling' character of its attractions, when at its supposed finest, precludes that. I was once favoured with half a dozen single bottles of the very finest Hocks in ordinary commerce— wines, the cheapest of which would have 'stood you in,' as the old phrase went, some ten shillings a bottle at the old prices, and the dearest nearer a sovereign. Except for curiosity's sake, I would much rather have had a similar collection of good

second-class claret; and after the first two glasses
of each Rhine wine, it would have been no
sacrifice in me to leave all the rest to any
compotator.

In fact, despite the wonderful first taste of the
great 'Auslese' wines, I think both Hock and
Moselle best as beverage drinks; for in these lower
qualities, the overpowering and almost barbaric
volume of flavour does not occur, and they are
very fresh and pleasant quenchers, going well
with most sorts of food. In days when it was still
lawful to drink bottles of wine in the plural, I
should have said that a bottle of hock at dinner,
and a bottle of claret after it, was a decent and
moderate allowance, and likely, as one of Scott's
people allows of something else, 'to bring a
blessing with it.' But for finer purposes I should,
once more, regard them as chiefly curiosities; and
accordingly, they never figured largely in my
wine-lists.[1]

What has been said of Hock applies with little
change to Moselle. The wines of Ausonius's
favourite river have long had a deserved reputation for flowery flavour; unfortunately they
have—of late years and even decades—acquired
another, also well deserved but much less envi-
able, as being the most abominably 'faked' of all
real or pretended juices of the grape. Whether it
was partly due to green unknowing youth or not,

---

[1] *Sparkling* Hock I liked little, and never bought. The 'Cabinet
Sekt,' which the interesting tenant of Amerongen patronised so
strongly, was 'a very *German*' champagne.

I cannot say, but I certainly seem to remember a time when Sparkling Moselle, though apt to be a little over-sweet, was a pleasant and seemed a wholesome liquor. I once, in company with a friend, made a light but agreeable meal at Oxford in the time of fritillaries, on a bottle of it; one of those nice china vases full of ice, which looked like giant conjurors' eggcups; and some wafers. It also went excellently with a most opposite accompaniment, certain sardine sandwiches, which they then made very well at the 'Mitre.' But after 1870 the general curse of insincerity, overreachingness and fraud, which even such a prophet of prophets of their own as Nietzsche recognised as hanging on Germany, attacked with particular ferocity the banks of the river whose various charms and benefits—its beauty and its variety, its wine and its trout and its grayling—the poet sang fifteen hundred years ago. Sparkling Moselle became a thing to be very carefully chosen or avoided altogether; the 'floweriness' of both sparkling and still had a horrible suspicion of the laboratory; and I once attributed (the faculty not disagreeing) a persistent attack of an unpleasant kind to an unduly prolonged sampling of the lighter sorts. Nor did I ever much affect the loudly-trumpeted Berncastler Doktor. Still, I own that a really good Scharzhofberg is a very fine wine; and that some of the beverage kinds from Piesporter to Graacher are mighty refreshing. But it may be well to warn those who cellar it that light Moselle, when young, is very apt to *cloud*, though it should, if good, clear later.

By the way, is there any *red* Moselle?

For the *red* hocks, however, I must put in a word, both in justice to them and in charity to my fellow-creatures. They—not merely Assmanshäuser, which certainly is the best, but Walporzheimer, Ober-Ingelheimer and others—are specifics for insomnia after a fashion which seems to be very little known, even among the faculty. Many years ago, when I was doing night-work for the press, and even after I had given that up, when I was rather unusually hard run at day-work, I found sleep on the off-nights as well as the others in the former case, and often in the latter, not easy to obtain. I was not such a fool as to take drugs, and I found hot grog or (what is not in itself inefficacious) strong beer, conducive to an uncomfortable mouth, etc., in the morning when taken only a few hours before. But a large claret glass or small tumbler of red hock did the trick admirably, and without deferred discomfort.

Somewhat akin, I suppose, to these red Hocks are the still red champagnes, which are very rare in England, but are very nice wines, and quite unsurpassed for what doctors might call neurotic dyspepsia. I think they first came to my knowledge as prescribed for Prosper Mérimée in the illness which preceded his death: and after long looking for them in vain, I was lucky enough, some five-and-thirty years ago, to pick up, at the Army and Navy Stores, some still Red Verzenay of 1868. I have never seen any since in lists.

In the same bin with it once lay some Côte

Rôtie—more easily procurable with us, but not very commonly seen on English dinner-tables. Something of what was said in the first of these papers as to Hermitage extends to this, and to Châteauneuf du Pape, and to many other less famous red wines of the south of France. They were, I believe, special favourites with Victor Hugo; and there is a certain Hugonic character about them all, though it never, except in Hermitage itself, rises to anything that suggests the full inspiration of the *Châtiments* or the *Contemplations*. It is more congenial to the novels in prose.

Other oddments of France put themselves forward—Saint-Péray, very pleasing now and then for a change; red sparkling Burgundy, which as noted above, I never found to be a success; while white sparkling Bordeaux is an anti-natural perversity, the invention of which deserved Dante's circle of the fiery rain. Then there is Picardan, the northernmost wine of France and the worst. This I never admitted to my cellar, but I have drunk it. And there are some French wines, well spoken of by French writers, which I have never come across, such as *vin d'Arbois*, a growth, I think, of Franche-Comté, as to which I have in vain sought particulars.

The outsiders of the Peninsula I never cellared much, but have tried sometimes. White Port I must say I think nearly deserving of the curse above pronounced on sparkling claret; but the faculty occasionally prescribe it. Calcavell*os* (or -*a*), which our ancestors used to drink more than we do, can be grateful and comforting. I never found the light Bucellas, which was rather popular some years ago, very satisfactory; indeed, except Manzanilla and its kin, already spoken of, at one end of Spain, and white Rioja (a capital beverage liquor) at the the other, the very light wines of the Iberian soil are to me rather suspect. I remember the dysentery after Najara, a story oddly confirmed by a mining engineer whom I met once in a hotel smoking-room, and who told me that his English miners, in much the same district of Spain, always suffered from that unpleasant complaint if they drank the common country wines. But I once drank a kind of Portuguese claret or Burgundy (was it called 'Priorato'?) which was far from contemptible. Tent and Alicant seem never now to be used with us for profane purposes; and I will not discuss Tarragona except to observe that in our present wine-famine it appears to have been promoted from that name to 'Spanish Port,' and from some half-crown an imperial quart to five shillings a bottle. But how many of my readers know Ampurdam? I never met it except long ago in the Channel Islands, where it was common. It looked and tasted rather like the curious compound called 'matrimony,' which the thrifty throats of the earlier nineteenth century used to consume. Few decent middle-class households then were without their standing decanters of port and sherry, which, when the port was getting rather stale, were mixed together as remnants, and so nothing was lost. When Ampurdam (which is an

63

actual place name) was new, it was very fiery and
rather diagreeable, standing to Port itself much as
Picardan does to Sherry. But at fifty or sixty years
old it became by no means despicable.

The word 'Iberian' was used just now from a
memory of a phrase of Thackeray's, 'Iberian or
Trinacrian wine,' and 'Trinacrian' of course
leads us straight to Marsala. I cannot say that I
have much personal affection for this wine,
despite all the literary and historical associations
of Sicily from Theocritus to Nelson. But it has
with me merits of early use (see chap. I); it was
probably the first wine that I tasted. At one time,
too, I was allowed to save occasional glasses of it
for the purpose (illegal, I suppose) of attempting
to distil brandy in one of my retorts—for, like
many other boys, I used to play at chemistry. The
illicit result, I remember, was far from intoxicating and very nasty. The best wine of the Marsala
class that I ever drank was some brown Syracuse
that we used to get in Guernsey; it might have
passed for a very rich, but by no means very
coarse, brown sherry. The dry Marsalas are often
fearfully acid. But on the whole the pleasantest
association I have with this wine dates quite
recently, from the actual disappearance of my
cellar itself. I had, for some special purpose,
procured a gallon jar of Marsala from one of the
big Stores, but had used very little of it. When the
sale was over, and bins of odd bottles of the best
ports for the last forty years had fetched something like a couple of pounds a dozen, this
despised vessel, not above three-quarters full,

went for more shillings than it had cost when it was untapped. It was (worse luck for me) before the war—though its first year was over—had brought about the present preposterous prices of wine; and these anomalies are characteristic of auctions. But when I see Marsala quoted at sixty, seventy, and eighty shillings a dozen, I say, 'Well, at any rate, this one wine did make *me* a profiteer!'

Of colonial wines I need not speak; for they hardly figure in my book at all; while I never drank any American. The great irruption of Greek and Hungarian kinds occurred before my time of collection, though at Oxford and afterwards I tried a certain number. The Greek were, as a rule, insufferably beastly. When, many years after, I happened to read Folengo's admirable description of the wine which 'ventris penetralia *raspat*,' I recognised their quality at once. You could not say this of Hungarian, even putting aside Tokay, which itself will probably never recover the disappearance of those Hapsburgs, with whom it was so inseparably connected. Republican Tokay would be a contradiction in terms. But to tell the truth, it never was a wine: only a prince of liqueurs. The commoner vintages were not intolerable; you *could* drink Carlowitz if you tried, and the Austrian Vöslauer was not to be despised. But I never quite got over a scientific lecturer, who contended that the chemical analysis of Château Lafite and that of some Hungarian *ordinaire* being quite the same (at least he said so), it was absurd to give five pounds a dozen for the one when you could get the other for twenty shillings. He was probably the spiritual father of the gentleman who told us the other day, after much orthodox experiment, that drinking without eating really made you more drunk than drinking with or after eating.

As to Italian, I suppose it does not travel well, though Chianti, like Carlowitz, can be drunk. I remember some very 'wersh' sparkling Asti; but I think I preferred it to some sparkling Lacrima Cristi, which suggested ginger beer alternately stirred up with a stick of chocolate and a large sulphur match. However, none of the things mentioned since Marsala ever figured in the cellar whose memoirs I have been summarising; indeed, I should have held most of them un-worthy of it. So let us wish it—at least as regards its most dignified contents—good-bye. I really think it was lovely and pleasant in its life, and the memory of it borrows its own bouquet and flavour. Many bottles went into it full, and came out empty or to be emptied. I only wish I could have used the empties, especially the jeroboams, in the pelting of any Pussyfoot who would make our dinner-tables dry places, and deprive our hearts of that which God sends to make them glad. Of some other good creatures which kept the wine company and of things connected with the cellar itself and the whole subject we may yet speak.

But, before passing to these, it may be right, since they have sometimes, though not often or largely, found a home with their betters, to mention those generally poor things, 'British

Wines.' I say 'generally,' because I have known ginger wine which was not a despicable liquor. A good Oxford man and good country clergyman, who was a very old friend of my family, and in whose house I more than once found hospitality, instruction and on one occasion my first acquaintance with the *Oxford and Cambridge Magazine*, used to have some made at home, which he called his 'sermon-writing essence,' and which was capital. And another person whom I could trust, my friend Mr. E. B. Michell, mildest-mannered of men, great with fist and scull, and one of the last of falconers before the Lord, told me that a tenant of his father's used to make rhubarb wine which was really worth drinking. 'Raisin wine' can be doctored into something not unlike a coarse Tent; and 'orange' into something by no means distantly suggestive of sherry and bitters. But all these are amiable 'fakings,' brandy being the chief accessory to the fact. 'Currant' *is* a poor creature—a dreadfully poor creature, though consecrated by the baby lover at the Holly Tree Inn—and as for 'cowslip,' I should wish it kept for the less Arcadian Arcadia. Of elder wine, though it need not be actually and immediately nasty, I am bound to say that, when I think of it, I always think likewise of the West Indian prelate who related his experience with some too hospitable members of his flock. 'They gave me,' he said, 'some wine—very nice wine; and then some cigars—very nice cigars. I think that, later, we had some rum—very nice rum. But, do you know,' and one can imagine the innocence of the pontifical smile, 'that afterwards I was positively *ill.*'[1]

Of English or Welsh grown wine that would really *be* wine—grape-juice glorified—if it could, I have spoken in a note to my *History of the French Novel*.[2] Whether anybody else has emulated the late Lord Bute in the trouble he took to introduce or revive this, I do not know. But judging from an experience of the actual Vinum Buteanum, I should say that a decent Marsala (and as will have been seen, I do not rank Marsala very high) was far preferable.

Miscellaneous notes on the last six chapters.

Before quitting the subject of wine proper, there are a few omitted points on which I may be permitted to say a word or two 'promiscuous,' as the vulgar have it.

It may seem odd that I have said nothing, in the chapter on Champagne, as to Saumur, Vouvray, and the Swiss imitations. These last I have never drunk. As to the first, I should feel inclined to borrow the saying of the innocent accomplice to whom a villain had imparted a share of stolen Champagne. Interrogated as to the various liquors which had been given to him, he said that there was one which was 'like ginger-beer, but not so nice.' If he had said this of Saumur I should not have found much fault with

[1] I believe elder wine can be made less deleterious by putting an equal quantity of brandy in it. But why not drink the brandy by itself?

[2] In connection (*v. sup.*) with Picardan.

him. Vouvray has not the same coarseness, but seems to me feeble.

I wonder if there exists anywhere a bottle of the old original Constantia? I am happy to say that in my youth I once drank it. (I am sorry for anyone who has not, once at least, drunk both real Constantia and real Tokay.) It has not, I believe, been made for many decades, the modern products of the vineyards so called being quite different. But it was of the sort to last. The late Bishop Creighton, who when vicar of Embleton in Northumberland was permitted to sample the famous Trevelyan cellar before it was committed to the sacrilegious hands of Dr. Richardson, fully confirmed my ideas as to white wines lasting much longer than red. And it is at least said that the stronger Rhenish and Bavarian wines will keep for centuries.

Old West Indians used to hold that Madeira ought to be drunk not merely *warmed* but *warm* in this climate; I suppose as a sort of restoration of the conditions to which it was accustomed.

At the time of the Champagne riots not long before the war, I asked a wine merchant of large experience whether it would not be possible to import the products of the outlying districts of the province—seeing that their discontent at the absorption of these products by the shippers of Reims, Epernay, etc., and the re-sale at much higher prices, led to the trouble—and to sell them as such. He answered that no merchant would dare to do it, the public being so much under the thrall of names that the stock would be left on the hands of anyone who did. If, as one suspects, the curious secondary firm-names under which some of these great shippers used to send out wines, cheaper than their official *cuvées*, covered outliers of this kind, they were sometimes excellent. But, in fact, no liquors required greater care than Champagnes at 60s. or 70s. per dozen before the war. They could in some cases be fit to put before anybody: in others it would be unpleasant to give a definition of fitness in the person who deserved to be set down to *them*.

I was doubtful, in writing the Claret chapter, as to saying something about the rather frequently discussed question of the official classification of Bordeaux wines, and its relation to their merits 'as it strikes a contemporary' foreigner. Perhaps a few words may be added. No one, I suppose, would turn out any of the three (or, if you admit Haut Brion, *four*) 'firsts.' The most popular promotion from the second class would no doubt be Mouton Rothschild, and from what I have said above, it will be pretty clear that I should not, in that position of examiner which I have so often held in other matters, be eager to blackball. But the very same difficulty which so often occurs in the other cases referred to presents itself here. If Mouton Rothschild is to have its first, why not Rauzan? If Rauzan, why not Léoville, which, as noted above, Anthony Trollope thought pure nectar? If these two, why not Pichon-Longueville, which in at least one instance I have known superlative? Once, too, I should have put before even these four that

Larose which some have called 'the lady of clarets,' which Thackeray in his early days made 'Sawedwardgeorgeearllyttonbulwig' couple with Lafite as a guess for his host's weally nectaweous wine; and which he later selected as Mr. Pendennis's best, wickedly wasted by clumsy Philip. But for many years I sought in vain for a Larose that was quite up to its old mark. So much for 'seconds,' though more might be said of them. But, sifting the thirds, why, one may say, should Lagrange, Langoa and Palmer be definitely postponed to Cos d'Estournel and Ducru-Beaucaillou? Descend further, and I at least should say that Beychevelle, by no means once in a way only, has been the equal of any third and some seconds, though it is only classed as a fourth; while of its actual class-fellows I hardly know one that is better to my knowledge than Mouton d'Armailhac, a fifth. Lastly, to go beyond the class-list in one instance only, why is that charming wine Château Citran 'gulfed'? But of wrangling about this (as about all class-lists without exception) there were no end.[1]

---

[1] Something may be expected on the question—What, if anything, should be taken and eaten with after-dinner wine? I am afraid that the 'whets' of our ancestors were rather stimulants to drinking (which nobody but an abstainer or a drunkard should require) than meliorants of appreciation. Their chief modern representatives—olives and devilled biscuits—are not bad, but I have never, despite a due devotion to Pallas, been such an enthusiast for the olive as some of my friends. And the *devilled* biscuit, a capital thing in itself, is rather violent for a fine wine. Plain Passover bread, or those 'Thin Captains,' which somewhat resemble it, seem to me best of all. Nuts pass, of course, but most 'soft' fruit is questionable. Grapes go not ill, but I have sometimes

felt a moral qualm, in marrying a grape too nearly to what is in a way its grandmother. Some accept peaches and nectarines; I rather doubt, though I am very fond of the latter. Strawberries have many votes, and some good stories, in their favour. But the one fruit which seems to me to go best with *all* wine, from hock to sherry and from claret to port, is the medlar—an admirable and distinguished thing in and by itself, and a worthy mate for the best of liquors.

CHAPTER VII

SPIRITS—HOLLANDS AND WHISKY

THERE is perhaps no division of any cellar, past or present, actual or possible, which to-day excites in the mind of a pious pilgrim to Lantern-Land such mixed feelings as that devoted to the produce of fermentation *plus* distillation. And when fond memory brings the other light of other days before him, the pilgrim must be a man of most angelic mildness if the predominating element of the mixture is not something like indignation. The present writer was informed, not long before the war broke out, by *two* trustworthy experts, that eighteen pence a gallon or threepence a bottle was an outside and indeed extravagant cost to fix for everything concerned in the production of most excellent spirit at proof. Now you get (when you *can* get it) stuff watered to 30° *under* proof at half a guinea. But let us, if possible, forget this tragedy, and return, if not to the blissful times and places elsewhere recorded, when and where you could buy a tumbler of Hollands for threepence, to more recent conditions, when in England and Scotland, excellent brandy cost five shillings a bottle; none but fancy or extra-old whiskies more than four; and gin, whether 'squareface' or London or Plymouth, not much more than half a crown.

When my cellar, if not exactly my cellar-book, was started, I had recently returned from a two years' sojourn in the north of Scotland, where, it is needless to say, I had become something of a judge of whisky; and the loss of the unblended product, direct from the Morayshire distilleries, was a real privation. I had never cared, and do not to this day care, much for the advertised blends, which, for this or that reason the public likes, or thinks it likes. And it was then difficult to get any other in London; a personal friend, himself a distiller, who allowed me to have some of his ware 'neat,' begged me not to mention the fact, as he was under a sort of contract only to supply the big middlemen. So for some time, though, of course, I always kept some whisky going, I did not drink much. Fortunately I had acquired in Guernsey, and not lost in Scotland, a taste for Hollands, which was easily procurable, and of which thenceforward my cellar was never destitute, till, at the final sale, I was fool enough to part with half a small cask-full for about seventeen shillings a gallon, not much over the price that it was to fetch per bottle two or three years later.

The British cellar-owner of the upper and middle classes at the present day does not as a rule

know much about Hollands; but it is a very excellent, most wholesome, and, at its best, most
palatable drink. It is true that it varies very con-
siderably; and its flavour is so pronounced that
some people can never reconcile themselves to it,
while others, who have liked it, lose the taste. The
most frequently met with and best known—De
Kuyper's, familiarly denominated 'J. D. K. Z.'
or 'square-face' simply—requires great age to
mature it, and, as generally sold, is rather harsh
and fiery. Wynand Fockink is more expensive,
but always to be trusted; its stone *litre*-jars reposed
and were replaced for many a year in my cellar.
Bols, like Wynand Fockink best known to us for
liqueurs, is also a sure card, and also rather dear.
Two excellent shipping firms, from whom I often
filled bins and casks, were Collings and Maingay
(both pure Guernsey names, but established in
Holland), whose gin I obtained from two different merchants in Plymouth and in Edinburgh,
but never saw elsewhere, and Jansen's, on which
latterly in Edinburgh I chiefly depended. But the
very best Hollands I ever had in my life had gone
through unusual experiences. It will be remembered that, a good many years ago, a man-of-war
(the name of which has slipped my memory) was
wrecked between Malta and Gozo. After a
considerable time her contents were salved, and
certain cases of Hollands, which had been supplied by Messrs. Collier, of Plymouth, were taken
back by them. Naturally, some bottles were
spoiled; and the curious corn-husks (rye or buck-
wheat?) in which they are usually packed had

suffered. But where the corks had held, the waters of 'the tideless, dolorous, midland sea' had proved themselves kind foster-mothers, and the gin was the softest and mellowest I ever tasted. Messrs. Collier were good-natured enough to let me have a case, in which I think not more than one or two bottles had suffered the worser 'sea-change,' and been ousted, while all the rest had undergone the better and remained. I wish I had had twenty cases instead of one.

But though I never deserted Schiedam, and, when I was ordered off claret about 1905, established a little stock-cask thereof, it was inevitable that, having returned to Scotland ten years earlier, I should revert to the 'wine of the country,' and should increase my relative consumption at the same catastrophe. The people who buy a bottle of 'Green Rhinoceros' or 'Purple and Yellow' as they want it, and are satisfied with that, though no doubt they might drink much worse liquor, know little about whisky. Nor do those who think that very old whisky is necessarily very good whisky know much more. One of those grocer-merchants, who dispense good liquor in the Northern Kingdom, and who sometimes have as much as a hundred thousand gallons stacked in their own bonded warehouses, once told me in confidence that he didn't himself care for *any* whisky that had been kept by itself in cask for more than fifteen years. 'It gets *slimy*,' he said; and I am bound to say I agree with him. In bottle, of course, it escapes that fate; but then there it hardly improves at all. The more excellent way—

formerly practised by all persons of some sense and some means north of the Tweed—is to establish a cask of whatever size your purse and your cellar will admit, from a butt to an 'octave' (14 gallons), or an 'anker' (ten), or even less; fill it up with good and drinkable whisky from six to eight years old, stand it up on end, tap it half-way down or even a little higher, and, when you get to or near the tap, fill it up again with whisky fit to drink, but not *too* old. You thus establish what is called in the sense of sherry a '*solera*,' in which the constantly aging character of the old constituents doctors the new accessions, and in which these in turn freshen and strengthen the old. 'It should be pretty good,' said a host of mine once in a country house beyond the Forth, 'it comes from a hundred-gallon cask, which has never been empty for a hundred years.' This is the state of the blessed, to which all cannot attain. But with care and judgment it can be be approached on quite a modest scale. I have done it in octaves for both Scotch and Irish whisky, and in ankers for Hollands and brandy, during such time as was allowed me. I think of their fair round proportions now with unsoured fondness.

The prettiest cask, however beautifully varnished (a process which I venture to think an error, for it must check the natural perspiration of the wood) and adorned with the most exquisitely silvered tap, will not turn bad whisky into good; and it is time to discuss the varieties of this admirable liquor in both its forms, wherein 'Scotus,' to alter Claudian's juxtaposition '*æmulat*

Iernen.' There once for a time was 'Welsh' whisky, manufactured, I suppose, under a mistaken belief that Celtic surroundings would suffice, but we will not reason of it, only mention it and pass. Transatlantic varieties, now threatened with extinction, may have a note later. For my own part, I am as impartial as an Englishman should be, and can afford to be in this instance, between *the* Two. Indeed, I used, while it was still possible for persons not millionaires or miners to do so, to drink one at lunch and the other at dinner, completing the 'Quis separabit?' with English gin at night. But I think it must be allowed that the 'Scotch drink' has more numerous and more delicate *varieties* of character than the Irish.

When I lived in Scotland the total number of distilleries was said, I think, to exceed two—certainly one—hundred; though not a few of the smaller were not working, as a consequence of the great whisky 'crash' of some years earlier. Morayshire alone, the non-metropolitan county which I once knew best, had some scores. But a good many, especially in the south, dealt with grain spirit, and I am speaking only of malt.[1] Taking all those that I have tried, I should say that some certainly stand above the rest. I used to endeavour to supply my cask with, and to keep independent jars of, the following:—Clyne Lish,

[1] With *one* more recent exception, the Whisky Commission of some years since was perhaps the most futile Commission on record, though it was not so mischievous as its successor. 'Grain' *is* only good for blending, or for mere 'drinkers for *drunkee*.'

Smith's Glenlivet (half the distilleries along and about the Spey from Grantown to the sea tack on the famous Glen to their own names, but 'Smith's' is the accepted premier), Glen Grant, Talisker, and one of the Islay brands — Lagavulin, Ardbeg, Caol Isla, etc. The picturesquely named 'Long John,' otherwise Ben Nevis, is less definite in flavour than any of these, but blends very well. Glendronach, an Aberdeenshire whisky, of which I did not think much forty years ago, improved greatly later; and I used to try both of these in my cask. But I always kept separate supplies of all, and amused myself with these, alone or variously blended, at intervals. A friend of mine from Oxford days, now dead, held some mixed Clyne Lish and Glenlivet of mine to be the best whisky he had ever drunk.

In conclusion, I think I have noticed, in the forty-five years since I began to study whisky, that the general style of most if not all kinds has changed, owing to the comparative disuse of 'toddy,' and the substitution of whisky-and-soda, or potash. The older whiskies were darker in colour, from being kept in golden sherry or madeira casks, rather sweeter in taste, and rather heavier in texture; the newer are 'lighter' in both the first and the last respect, and much drier in taste. But the abominable tyranny of enforced 'breaking down' to thirty below proof has spoilt the ethers of the older whiskies terribly.

There is, as indeed I have hinted, no 'wrong to Ireland' intended in not noticing its produce first. I have postponed it, not that I love it less, but because I do not know quite so much about it. I have never *lived* in Ireland, only spending there a few 'B.B.B.' days, as they say on the placards of dissenting chapels (I extend these in the case mentioned to 'Brief, Bright and *Beatific*'), and though I have tried a fair number of Irish whiskies, and have never been without some, they are much fewer than the Caledonian brands. My book contains entries of both the Jamesons, John and William; of Roe, Power, and E. and J. Burke from Dublin; of Persse and another unnamed from Galway; of Coleraine, Comber, and one or two not named from Belfast and the north; and of some (good but not further identified) from Cork. (I may mention by the way that the very best Irish whisky I ever remember, which was given me by my old friend Colonel Welman, Brigade-Major in Guernsey many years ago, also came from Cork.) There may have been one or two others, but these were what I chiefly 'kept going.' Of their respective characters I have not much to say. Irish whisky wants, I think, more keeping than Scotch, and the famous 'J.J.' especially is seldom thoroughly good before it is ten years old. Some of the best I ever had was some *William* Jameson of nearly twenty. But when it is good, it has the national characteristic of being (with the same limitation) singularly ingratiating. No spirit makes you appreciate so fully that beautiful line,

And the soft wings of Peace cover him round

which Marryat (or Howard) unwittingly illustrated by the incident of Rattlin the Reefer being

sheltered from the stramash on the harbour of
Cork itself in the embraces of the Misses O'Toole.
Scandal has said that it sometimes crosses the
larger bay outside and returns as Cognac.
Whether there ever was any truth in this, I cannot
say: A charming poem on this new 'Return of the
Wild Geese' might be written. But it is literally
true that on two different occasions I myself,
whose palate is not, as perhaps these pages may
show, quite unexercised in such things, have
taken what was supposed to be brandy for Irish
whisky.

Of Canadian and American whiskies I have
promised a notice, but shall not say much, though
my cellar has seen several. Walker's well-known
Canadian Club is the least unpalatable that I
have tried; though for some samples of American
I have given more money than I ever paid in the
good days for the best of the home brands. It was
said, I think, in the whisky enquiries of some years
ago, that the high colour and strong flavour of
these spirits is due to the practice of singeing the
insides of the casks. It may be so or may not. But
the real fact is that the American, if not the
Canadian kinds, are obviously prepared for
drinking as liqueurs or cocktails, not for mixing.
As such they are not repulsive; they are less good,
but not loathsome, as rather sweet toddy; very
nasty with cold water; and worse with soda or
potash. That they are or were generally drunk
'neat' is, I believe, the fact; and if any rational
comparison of the state of America and England
in regard to alcoholic liquor were made, this fact

81

would have to be taken into 'high consideration.'

Notes on Toddy.—This, even in Scotland, now almost prehistoric compound ought to be made, according to Morayshire rules, in a fashion opposite to that usually imagined to be correct. You put in the hot water, sweetened to taste, first, and let the sugar melt thoroughly; *then* you add the whisky. And, of course, you do not 'swig' it brutally from the rummer or tumbler, but ladle it genteelly, as required, with a special instrument made and provided for the purpose, into a wine-glass which has been brought, again specially inverted beforehand in the rummer or tumbler itself.

CHAPTER VIII

SPIRITS—BRANDY, RUM AND GIN,
WITH SOME EXOTIC THINGS

BRANDY is, no doubt, in a certain sense—even in
more than one—the most excellent of spirits—
'Aqua *Vitae*' by excellence. It comes, to speak
scholastically, from the noblest source—the
grape. It passes through the most dignified stages,
for it is wine before it is brandy, and therefore
presumably drinkable, while I do not envy
anyone who drinks the initial forms of whisky,
'feints' and 'forshotts,' though the latter (as to the
spelling of which I confess doubts) is remarkably
good as an embrocation for rheumatism. It is the
object of the most reverential treatment; for
residents in the district say that the small farmers
who distil it do not part with their older treasures
without personal reluctance. And whether it is
the most pleasantly drinkable or not (I own that I
myself get much sooner tired of brandy and soda
than of whisky and potash) it can acquire as a
liqueur the finest flavour, and is unapproached as

a medicine. All alcoholic drinks, rightly used,[1] are good for body and soul alike; but as a restorative of both there is nothing like brandy.

Like other excellent things, however, it does not admit of much talking. There is good brandy, and there is, though it is almost a contradiction in terms, bad brandy; but there is no great variety in the good, except that produced by purity and age. Outward differences, of course, there are; and a few of origin and kind. As far as the latter are concerned, the decree has long gone forth that all brandy—at least all French brandy—is to be *called* Cognac; though how much of it actually comes from the Charente is quite another question. 'Armagnac' brandy, a genuine place-name with an interesting historical association (you may drink Armagnac after Burgundy now and they won't quarrel) used to be honestly sold in the Channel Islands as such. I never saw it quoted or offered in England. 'Eau de Vie de Marc,' a sort distilled from grape husks as well as juice, is sometimes procurable, and not to be despised as a liqueur, though it does not 'mix' well. I have had it in my cellar. Not there, nor in England at all, have I seen rose-coloured brandy as I have in French country districts. But like all other spirits it is of course originally white, and I have myself possessed some of that.[2] With us, as those who

[1] Even absinthe, the most open to abuse, is sovereign sometimes, as for instance, after sea-sickness.

[2] It is curious that gin is the only spirit that has as a rule been allowed to remain white, except in such cases as 'raspberry gin,' which was popular in the eighteenth century, and 'clove gin,'

know a little about the history of the subject are aware, 'Pale' brandy, which is now the rule, was something of an exception till about the middle of the nineteenth century. 'Brown' is perhaps now taking its place as such. I always kept some brown brandy in my cellar, for it is better as a liqueur than pale, and very much better for the composition of that grand old stuff beloved of Mr. Pickwick, and doubtless part-cause of his virtues—hot brandy and water. But with soda water it is a mistake, and I trust that another great man in fiction (which is only another kind of fact), Dr. Opimian, of whom it is recorded that he took his brandy at night with hot water in winter and soda water in summer, provided for the difference. He was certainly right in preferring brandy at this time. Indeed, the three spirits noticed in this chapter have an advantage over those of the last chapter as 'nightcaps.' Whisky has a tendency to keep the drinker of it, except in rather immoderate quantities, awake.[1]

---

which I never saw, but which I suppose must have taken some colour as well as taste from the spice. I have noted above white rum and white brandy, but not, I think, white whisky, which however is quite to be mentioned 'for the sake of honour.' I have drunk it in Scotland, and have had it of excellent quality from Bristol. But I think the best that I ever drank was at the Ulster Club in Belfast, a hospitable institution fit to be adorned with various laurels. It stands to reason that whisky left in such a condition will be drier than that which has been casked in succession to anything but the driest sherry. And I own I think dryness a great merit in Scotch if not in Irish usquebaugh or 'scuback,' as the French were wont to *estropier* the word brought by Jacobite exiles from the two whisky countries. Hollands, especially when very old, is often straw-coloured.

[1] In the text I thought it well not to couple non-French brandy

It was most pleasant, during the late war, to read the unvarying testimony of all qualified and unprejudiced authorities to the invaluable services of the rum ration, which, in defiance of fanaticism and in compliance with common sense and experience, was issued to our men. The merits, virtues and interests of rum are very great and unusually various. That it is 'good for de tomac,' as it (under a false name, to be sure) was of yore asserted to be on a famous occasion, may be unhesitatingly asserted and countersigned. It is certainly the most carminative and comforting of all spirits. Everybody knows that hot rum and water is sovereign for a cold, but perhaps everybody does not know exactly how the remedy should be applied. This is the *probatum*. You must take it in bed; premature consumption merely wastes the good creature. It should be made, in a large rummer-glass, as hot as you can drink it (hence the advice of the rummer—for a mere tumbler may burn your hands), not too sweet, but

with French. But for completeness others, some of them not despicable, should perhaps be mentioned here. Of 'British' brandy I have known little (at least of what called itself so), and have not desired much further acquaintance. But I should like just to have tasted the formidable specimen possessed by the great Mr. Moulder in *Orley Farm*. Australian I used to drink occasionally for some years as an economy, and it is not bad; but after a time I got tired of it. Spanish can be very good. I do not desire anything much better than Domecq's 'Fundador' of 1874; though perhaps by this time it may suggest the caution of a candid wine-merchant as to 'Waterloo' Sherry. 'We call it so; but I cannot undertake to state mathematically the proportion of 1815 in it.' Even the lesser degrees of this brandy—bearing 'vines' instead of 'stars' as badges—can be well spoken of.

so strong that you sink back at once on the pillow, resigning the glass to the ready hands of a sympathising bedside attendant, preferably feminine. If you do not wake the next morning, possibly with a slight headache but otherwise restored, there must be something really the matter with you.[1] And it must never be forgotten that without rum that glorious liquor called punch — that liquor 'nowhere spoken against in the Scriptures' — that wine of midnight — cannot really exist. Brandy punch (though in perfect punch there *should* be brandy), whisky punch, gin punch are all misnomers. 'No bishop, no king' is a wise maxim; but (for there have been kingdoms which were not Christian) it is not such an eternal verity as, 'No rum, no punch.'

The most remarkable rum I ever possessed was some white or rather pale straw-coloured spirit, which I bought at a sale in Edinburgh; which had belonged to Wallace of Kelly, a somewhat 'legended' laird of the earlier nineteenth century; and which was said to have been cellared in or before 1845, my own birth-year (I had a little brandy of the same date once, but sacrificed all save a

---

[1] The feeble-minded or hypocritical may substitute 'sal volatile punch,' *i.e.* hartshorn, hot water, lemon and sugar. It is not bad, but far inferior to rum.

The recipe above intended for real punch is as follows: —three parts of rum, two of brandy ('Ensign O'Doherty' substitutes arrack), one of lemon juice, and six of hot water, the quantity of sugar being a matter quite of taste. I never knew this mixture found fault with by respectable persons of any age, sex or condition, from undergraduates to old ladies, at any hour between sunset and sunrise.

87

thimbleful of it to pious purposes under stress of Dora the Detestable). It was still excellent with hot water, but was perhaps best as a liqueur, though it may have been rather too tarry for some tastes. Precious, too, was some Wedderburn of 1870 which I used to get from my friends Messrs. Harvey, and which was not the less agreeable because 1870 itself was the first year in which I ever abode, for more than a few hours, by the gorge of the Avon. But I cannot help regretting the darker rums of older days: nearly all rum is pale now. The dark rum certainly *looked* better when diluted: and the eyes have a right to be pleased as well as the palate. I think its flavour was fuller too, and allied itself better with that of its constant friend the lemon. It is asserted, with what truth I know not, that the methods of distillation have altered. But it is still famously good; we could repair much of our long injustice to the West Indies by drinking more of it; it is quite free from the hypocritical but colourable objection that the making of it wastes food-stuffs—indeed the more rum the more sugar — and if we ever get fair taxation and uncontrolled trade again it might be quite cheap. I have often wished to drink Java and Queensland rum, but have never been able to get hold of either, though I have seen some good-looking dark Australian stuff in the Tantalus-case of an Exhibition.

Nor have I ever disdained the humble and much reviled liquid which is the most specially English of all spirits; which, as observed before,

you used to be able to procure at its best for not
much more than half-a-crown a bottle; and which
now, owing to the witchcrafts and (for I must be
permitted biblical freedom) whoredoms of 'Dora'
with persons unnecessary to mention,[1] has recently cost half-a-guinea. I have always been
sorry for gin. By popular abbreviation from
'Geneva' (itself a corruption of the still prettier
genièvre) it acquired a name which is unfairly
suggestive of traps and snares. First the neglect,
and then as usual the hasty action, of the
legislature brought it into extreme discredit
nearly two hundred years ago; and Hogarth, one
of the best of artists and fellows, but not precisely
of thinkers, made that bad name worse. Further
neglect and further stupidity saddled it with the
odious association of 'gin palace'; and the ir-
rational opprobrium actually reached such a
height a hundred years ago that even men who
represented themselves in the *Noctes Ambrosianae*,
as drinking oceans of whisky, upbraided Hazlitt
for drinking gin; while, not far from the end of the
nineteenth century, Anthony Trollope by no
means caricatured fact when he made, in *Ayala's
Angel*, a vapourish girl be shocked because her
uncle, host and practically saviour from des-
titution, drank gin and water in place of the port
which he had to give up to meet the expenses of
her stay.

Now there is no more real reason for all this

---

[1] The young man in Tennyson's poem was rather a feeble person;
but he showed a prophetic strain of wisdom in saying 'I *will* not
marry Dora.'

obloquy than there is for abusing water because the Inquisitors employed the water-torture, or because pirates and Bolshevists have made people 'walk the plank.' No doubt there is bad gin. I daresay the gin that was drunk in Gin Lane at a penny a glass was rather terrible. Its very powerful flavour masks adulteration rather easily; and I daresay again that which was sold 'for drunkee' was vilely doctored. But to continue the argument used just now, people have committed hideous crimes with razors and pocket-knives, and both these implements, as well as many others, have been forged and sold by honest persons though they were made of worthless steel. 'In its natural and healthy condition,' as Lamb said of the above-mentioned Hazlitt (and as, for he was fond of it, he might have said of actual gin itself) gin is a capital spirit. When well made both its taste and its odour are very agreeable; it is admittedly one of the most wholesome of all the clan, and a real specific for some kinds of disease. There is perhaps no liquor more suitable for hot weather than gin and soda with a slice of lemon—'the British soldier's delight,' as they used to call it in the barracks where I stayed in the sixties; and though I was obliged to call gin-punch a misnomer as an appellation, I should not much mind how cold I was if I could have a good tumbler of it to dispel my shivers.

There is not very much to say about different kinds of gin, though almost every distiller or refiner of it has fancy flavourings of his own. As it *is* 'refined,' and not simply distilled, it gains little

if anything from age; and if the Northern Cobbler
had broken down and tasted his big bottle, I do
not know that he would have found it as 'meller'
as he expected. But when good it is a good
creature always. I used generally to keep three
kinds of it—'Old Tom,' the sweeter and heavier
variety; 'unsweetened London,' which seems to
me the best gin-of-all-work; and 'Plymouth,' the
most delicate in flavour and perhaps the whole-
somest. Some gins, though I do not want to
scandal their makers, strike me as over-flowery in
taste.

A few words may be added on some less
common spirits, which I have had from time to
time in bin or on shelf. Arrack, which at one time
seems to have been as common in English cellars
as brandy or rum, and much commoner than
whisky, is seldom seen now; and I once came just
too late for a Scotch one, which had been
ancestrally famous for it. What I have had in my
own possession was a not disagreeable cross
between rum and Irish whisky—good enough
neat, but better in the 'rack punch,' for which it
used to be chiefly employed, and which, at
Vauxhall, seems to have started enquiries whether
its name was derived from its alleged constituent,
or from its consequences next morning. The
Norwegian 'Aquavit,' which used to flow so freely
(*vide* that delightful book, *Forest Life: a
Fisherman's Sketches in Norway and Sweden*), but to
which styptics have been applied by modern
churlishness, seemed to me, in the specimens I

have had, a weak and not very delicious whisky, as indeed its older name of 'corn-brandy' implies. I think much better of its connection, Vodka — the most tragically associated of all liquids, for the absurd withholding of it probably had much to do with the Russian Revolution, while the inevitable reaction made that Revolution, when it came, more terrible. 'Raki,' which I suppose is like arrack, I never tried; nor 'plum spirit' — indigenous to the brave little country, which used to 'spell itself with a *we*,' and has not bettered the spelling more recently.[1]

---

[1] One note more, to the last chapter rather than to this. The atrocities of 'Dora' have naturally revived illicit distilling. It is said that some of the results are quite good. But although I consider the offence a natural consequence of the present persecution, I must confess that the only whisky of this kind that I ever drank was incredibly nasty.

CHAPTER IX

LIQUEURS

IT may perhaps have been noticed by anyone
who does me the honour to read this little book
that I am rather partial to alcoholic liquors. No
doubt they are bad things if you make yourself a
slave to them; but then most things to which you
make yourself a slave are bad—with some rare
exceptions in the case of women, and then only
because a few of them accept the slavery as
reciprocal. I could, if I chose, bid adieu to all
these liquors to-morrow without difficulty,
though with very great regret.[1] I have recently,

[1] As the late Mr. Leland put it—in language perhaps shocking
to those who read without understanding, but not to those who can
see the allegory—

> We'll get drunk among the roses,
> And lie sober on the straw.

Nor do those who have most enjoyed the roses and the wine take
the straw and the sobriety least philosophically. Or, if anyone's
nerves need more sentimental treatment, here is a variant on the
famous ballad-lament, for something had and lost, which will
apply in this meaner matter and in others:

and at various other times of my life, reduced my consumption to any desirable point. I think those who can drink them and do not, fools; but I think those who can't drink them and do, worse fools, and unjust men too, because they bring scandal on an excellent creature, and consume that share of it which should go to others.

All which is not padding, but a relevant introduction to what I am going to say of Liqueurs—that of all the various species of their genus they can be least unconditionally recommended. They are, save occasionally for medicinal purposes, the most positive of superfluities and extravagances.[1] They are also, being as a rule both too strong and too sweet, the most questionably wholesome; and excess in them results in sufferings the most unpleasant of all such sufferings. Nor do they possess the natural grace and charm—the almost intellectual as well as sensual interest—of the best wine. On the other hand, they are for the most part very pleasant to the taste; they are frequently very pretty to look at; and if there be any truth in the old and perhaps somewhat rash statement as to the connection

---

O! had I wist, before I kissed,
 That love would be sae sair to *gain*—
I had played the game, just all the same,
 To win the pleasure WITH the pain.

It has indeed been objected that this gives a discord on the minor key of the opening: but even the objector admitted that it was a right English mood and mode.

[1] Especially when people ask, as (it may be interesting to posterity to know) they sometimes are asking now, thirty shillings for a *half-*litre bottle of *yellow* Chartreuse.

between the wills or wishes of womankind and of the Divinity, they cannot be hateful to God. For nearly all ladies, and especially all young ladies, like them very much indeed. Also they have a good many other sorts of interest, from their great variety of kind and association. I never was myself much addicted to them, but I have usually had a bottle or two of a few of the best in my cellar while I had it.

Liqueurs are, as has just been said, extremely numerous; indeed, when I knew France (which as far as actual presence goes is a long time since, much too long for me to have had any chance of being useful there recently) almost every chemist in every small town had one of his own, which was sovereign for digestion and other things. Some of the less known ones had considerable merits: I remember a big bottle of 'Berrichonne' which was quite nice. But the best of these minorities was one called 'Génépi des Alpes,' which, having originally met it in those isles, favoured of Bacchus, which have been so often mentioned, I succeeded in procuring from these latter till the supply somehow stopped. Like that of the majority of these minorities, its flavour was of the Chartreuse class,[1] but less peculiar and powerful: and it was also much weaker as a spirit.

[1] Although I have not the slightest knowledge of botany, I am tempted (leaning mainly on the arm of my almost life-long friend, Sir W. T. Thiselton-Dyer, but absolving him from responsibility for any slips of my own natural and unscientific pravity) to venture a quasi-botanical note on the probable source of these flavours. It seems that the genus Artemisia (by the way, the French *armoise*

throws a twilight on the Goddess) contains four groups of very numerous species; but that all, or nearly all, the known flavourers of liquors belong to the group Absinthia; *A. Absinthium* itself being responsible for Absinthe and (partially?) for Chartreuse. *A. nevadensis* (see on Manzanilla) seems to be a variety of *A. camphorata*, a suggestive name; while *A. Barretieri*, another Spaniard, but of the Seraphidia group, is admittedly used for liqueur as well as for medicinal purposes. *A. mutellina* and *A. glacialis* supply Génépi: and I personally suspect them in Chartreuse. Of the other groups it is doubtful whether any flavours liqueurs, though the Dracunculi enrich cookery with Tarragon. The Abrotana or Southernwoods suggest capabilities in our way: but do not seem to be known flavourers. On the other hand *A. maritima*, one of the fourth group, or Seraphidia, is said by one 18th century authority to be 'an ingredient of distilled waters,' and by another (*c.* 1726) to be used by Dublin alehouse keepers ['When the early purl is done'] to make their purl with. One wonders whether there was *A. maritima* in the purl which refreshed Peter Simple after that agitating night with the press-gang and the Amazons?; whether George Borrow would have objected to sea-wormwood in purled beer as he did to worm-wood proper in plain ale?; and whether John Buncle, Esq., in those very days when he and his Dublin friends sang 'Let us go to Johnny Maclaine's, and see if his ale be good or no,' gave orders (the alehouse itself was by the sea-side) to have it purled with *A. maritima*—and plenty of gin? This last named plant and *A. sacrorum* (one of the southerwoods) Sir W. M. Conway found in the Himalayas; could an 'Eau *Sacrée* des Lamas' or 'Lamaseraïne' be made of them? In M. Levier's botanical promenade in the Caucasus I find only *A. campestris* var. *sericea* (one of the Tarragon group) and *A. splendens* noted as representing this Garden of Diana (some would say of Proserpine) there. Perhaps Prometheus foresaw the dangers of the Green Muse, and kept her from the scene of his torture and his triumph. Anyhow, the connection between mountains and liqueurs through the genus Artemisia is interesting, and an instance of the innumerable interests which alcohol lends to life. As such I have dwelt on it. My unwritten *History of Wine* would have dealt with the somewhat Chartreuse-suggesting Ἀψινθίτης οἶνος of the Greeks; and the question whether when Artemisia drank the ashes of Mausolus they tasted like wormwood; etc., etc. (Later kindness from Kew adds many Caucasian Artemisias *including* Absinthium.)

Of the recognised seductions that accompany coffee after dinner, I suppose Chartreuse itself and Curaçao have the best claims to be the kings of the Liqueurish Brentford. The rivals or imitations of the first-mentioned are, even excluding the humbler ones just referred to, very numerous. Benedictine; Trappistine; a certain 'Père Kermann,' which from a joke of mine about its legend-wrapper my children used to call 'Forty Years in the Wilderness'; a red Italian Chartreuse or Certosa (far from bad) and others will occur. But none of them approaches, for instruction in complexity and delight in appeal of flavour, the famous but now exiled preparation itself. And it must be *green*; there is no such absolutely veracious application of a well-known maxim as that all yellow Chartreuse would be green if it could. As might be expected from its character and composition, it improves enormously with age; I kept some once for fifteen or sixteen years to its huge advantage. At the same time there is always something rather severe about it; it is not so engaging as not too sweet, but also not too dry or 'thin' Curaçao. The very best of *this* amiable temptation that I ever possessed, or indeed that I ever drank, was some which used to be procurable at the well-known house of Justerini and Brooks in the vanished Opera Colonnade, between forty and fifty years ago. It also was green, but brown is perhaps the more germane colour, and white is not to be contemned merely for its whiteness. 'Grand Marnier,' the recent popular and expensive French variant on Curaçao, has never seemed to me quite its equal; but the Cape liqueur called Vanderhum is excellent.

To our grandfathers the chief companions or rivals of Curaçao were Maraschino and Noyau — both admirable things when they are not, as they both sometimes are, a trifle sickly. I think less ill of our Fourth king among my namesakes than some people do, but I cannot approve of his fancy for maraschino punch. It is a blunder and a confusion; nearly as bad as drinking Château Yquem with soda-water. But there is something very attractive in a maraschino *bottle* with its straw envelope. And Martinique can hold its own with Zara; though Noyau condescends sometimes to rouge itself, while the wares of Luxardo and Drioli remain stainless. The 'Water of Cherry' which in comparatively guiltless days the German made in his western districts, and the 'Water of Gold' which he devised in his eastern, are or were by no means bad things. I hope that the rather unsettled fate of Dantzic will not dry up the fount of Goldwasser, which pleased sight and smell and taste alike.

Still further eastward and with still unhappier recent local memories, comes Kümmel — I suppose the most wholesome of all liqueurs, and not far from the nicest. 'Ça pique dans le nez,' says one, I think, of M. Zola's young women; but certainly 'ça chatouille le palais.' 'Parfait Amour' is an older-fashioned drink, but, with the most careful protestation against any blasphemy of the name which it takes in vain, I cannot say that I think much of the thing. And as for Rosolio (I think it was Rosolio, but not the variety from which Samuel Titmarsh suffered), I have much too sharp a memory of once incautiously opening a bottle of it over a fire-place, so that the liquid dropped, and the flame catching it, ran up and scorched my arm, to meddle with it any more. All these, and not a few others—Cassis, Anisette, Crême de Menthe, 'Cointreau,' a pretty violet-coloured mixture from the Riviera which was popular some years ago, but of which I forget the name—have figured for a time on a certain shelf which I used to reserve for such things. But I have never possessed, drunk, seen, or in modern books heard of, 'Citron,' which the lady used to 'drink with His Grace and Chartres.' Does any-body know what it was? It sounds like a kind of Curaçao made with lemon or actual citron-peel instead of orange.

However, I will not close this short chapter without saying something of the supposed wick-edest of all the tribe—the 'Green Muse'—the Water of the Star Wormwood, whereof many men have died—the *absinthia tetra*, which are deemed to deserve the adjective in a worse sense than that which the greatest of Roman poets meant. I suppose (though I cannot say that it ever did me any) that absinthe has done a good deal of harm. Its principle is too potent, not to say too poisonous, to be let loose indiscriminately and intensively in the human frame. It was, I think, as a rule made fearfully strong, and nobody but the kind of lunatic whom it was supposed to produce, and who may be thought to have been destined to lunacy, would drink it 'neat.' Of its being so drunk I once had a harmless but very comic experience. The late Bishop Creighton and I had contiguous lodgings, during the later part of our undergraduate life at Oxford, in one of the old houses east of University and now destroyed. We used them practically in common, employing one sitting-room to eat and the other to work in. On one occasion we had had some men to dinner, and when the last went our good landlady, who had been hovering about on the landing in an agitated manner, rushed into the room crying, 'O! gentlemen, is that stuff poison?' We naturally requested further light. It turned out that a glass of absinthe, which had been poured out but not used, had been taken downstairs, and that our excellent landlord, sagely observing, as his wife rather reproachfully said, 'It *must* be good if the gentlemen drink it,' had quaffed it without water, but as she said 'as he would gin,' and had naturally found it rather too much for him. We calmed her fears and recommended a plentiful draught of water, adding in the most delicate way in the world, a caution that it was not invariably necessary to drink liquor that was left over; and dismissed her. Also we endeavoured—for Creighton was like Thackeray's Jones 'a fellow of very kind feeling, who afterwards went into the Church,' and I hope I was not less kind, though my destiny was more profane—not to laugh too much till she had closed the door.

A person who drinks absinthe neat deserves his fate whatever it may be. The flavour is concentrated to repulsiveness; the spirit burns 'like a torch-light procession'; you must have a preternaturally strong or fatally accustomed head if that head does not ache after it. Moreover, you lose all the ceremonial and etiquette which make the proper fashion of drinking it delightful to a man of taste. When you have stood the glass of liqueur in a tumbler as flat-bottomed as you can get, you should pour, or have poured for you, water gently into the absinthe itself, so that the mixture overflows from one vessel into the other. The way in which the deep emerald of the pure spirit clouds first into what would be the colour of a star-smaragd, if the Almighty had been pleased to complete the quartette of star-gems,[1] and then into opal; the thinning out of the opal itself as the operation goes on; and when the liqueur glass contains nothing but pure water and the drink is ready, the extraordinary combination of refreshingness and comforting character in odour and flavour—all these complete a very agreeable experience. Like other agreeable experiences it may no doubt be repeated too often. I never myself drank more than one absinthe in a day, and I have not drunk so much as one for some thirty years. But the Green Muse is *bonne diablesse* enough if you don't abuse her; and when you land

---

[1] As yet only a triad—sapphire (which is pretty common), ruby (rarer), and topaz, which I have never seen, and which the late Signor Giuliano, who used to be good enough to give me much good talk in return for very modest purchases, told me he had seen only once or twice. But an ordinary emerald in *cabochon* form, represents one of the stages of the diluted absinthe very fairly.

after rough handling by the ocean she picks you up as nothing else will.[1]

[1] The once home-made 'cordials'—Cherry Brandy, 'Gean' Whisky, Sloe Gin, and one or two others—are rather flavoured spirits than liqueurs; and much more wholesome than most of the foreign concoctions. There is a Copenhagen Cherry Brandy too, which deserves a good word.

CHAPTER X

BEER, CIDER, ETC.

THERE is no beverage which I have liked 'to live with' more than Beer; but I have never had a cellar large enough to accommodate much of it, or an establishment numerous enough to justify the accommodation. In the good days when servants expected beer, but did not expect to be treated otherwise than as servants, a cask or two was necessary; and persons who were 'quite' generally took care that the small beer they drank should be the same as that which they gave to their domestics, though they might have other sorts as well. For these better sorts at least the good old rule was, when you began on one cask always to have in another. Even Cobbett, whose belief in beer was the noblest feature in his character, allowed that it required *some* keeping. The curious 'white ale,' or *lober agol*—which, within the memory of man, used to exist in Devonshire and Cornwall, but which, even half a century ago, I have vainly sought there—was, I believe, drunk quite new; but then it was not pure malt and not hopped at all, but had eggs ('pullet-sperm in the brewage') and other foreign bodies in it.

I did once drink, at St. David's, ale so new that it frothed from the cask as creamily as if it had been bottled: and I wondered whether the famous beer of Bala, which Borrow found so good at his first visit and so bad at his second, had been like it.[1] On the other hand, the very best Bass I ever drank had had an exactly contrary experience. In the year 1875, when I was resident at Elgin, I and a friend now dead, the Procurator-Fiscal of the district, devoted the May 'Sacrament holidays,' which were then still kept in those remote parts, to a walking tour up the Findhorn and across to Loch Ness and Glen Urquhart. At the Freeburn Inn on the first-named river we found some beer of singular excellence: and, asking the damsel who waited on us about it, were informed that a cask of Bass had been put in during the previous October, but, owing to a sudden break in the weather and the departure of all visitors, had never been tapped till our arrival.

Beer of ordinary strength left too long in the cask gets 'hard' of course; but no one who deserves to drink it would drink it from anything but the

---

[1] This visit (in the early eighties) had another relish. The inn coffee-room had a copy of Mr. Freeman's book on the adjoining Cathedral, and this was copiously annotated in a beautiful and scholarly hand, but in a most virulent spirit. 'Why can't you call things by their plain names?' (in reference to the historian's Macaulayesque periphrases) etc. I have often wondered who the annotator was.

cask if he could help it. Jars are make-shifts,
though useful makeshifts: and small beer will not
keep in them for much more than a week. Nor are
the very small barrels, known by various affec-
tionate diminutives ('pin,' etc.) in the country
districts, much to be recommended. 'We'll drink
it in the *firkin*, my boy!' is the lowest admission in
point of volume that should be allowed. Of one
such firkin I have a pleasant memory and mem-
orial, though it never reposed in my *home* cellar. It
was just before the present century opened, and
some years before we Professors in Scotland had,
of our own motion and against considerable
opposition, given up half of the old six months'
holiday without asking for or receiving a penny
more salary. (I have since chuckled at the horror
and wrath with which Mr. Smillie and Mr.
Thomas would hear of such profligate conduct.)
One could therefore move about with fairly long
halts: and I had taken from a friend a house at
Abingdon for some time. So, though I could not
even then drink quite as much beer as I could
thirty years earlier a little higher up the Thames,
it became necessary to procure a cask. It came—
one of Bass's minor mildnesses—affectionately
labelled 'Mr. George Saintsbury. Full to the
bung.' I detached the card, and I believe I have it
to this day as my choicest (because quite un-
solicited) testimonial.

Very strong beer permits itself, of course, to be
bottled and kept in bottle: but I rather doubt
whether it also is not best from the wood; though
it is, equally of course, much easier to cellar it and

keep it bottled. Its kinds are various and curious.
'Scotch ale' is famous, and at its best (I never
drank better than Younger's) excellent: but its
tendency, I think, is to be too sweet. I once
invested in some—not Younger's—which I kept
for nearly sixteen years, and which was still
treacle at the end. Bass's No. 1 requires no praises.
Once when living in the Cambridgeshire village
mentioned earlier I had some, bottled in Cambridge itself, of great age and excellence. Indeed,
two guests, though both of them were Cambridge
men, and should have had what Mr. Lang once
called the 'robust' habits of that University, fell
into one ditch after partaking of it. (I own that the
lanes thereabouts are very dark.) In former days,
though probably not at present, you could often
find rather choice specimens of strong beer produced at small breweries in the country. I
remember such even in the Channel Islands. And
I suspect the Universities themselves have been
subject to 'declensions and fallings off.' I know
that in my undergraduate days at Merton we
always had proper beer-glasses, like the old 'flute'
champagnes, served regularly at cheese-time with
a most noble beer called 'Archdeacon,' which was
then actually brewed in the sacristy of the College
chapel. I have since—a slight sorrow to season
the joy of reinstatement there—been told that it
is now obtained from outside.[1] And All Souls is

[1] When I went up this March to help man the last ditch for Greek,
I happened to mention 'Archdeacon': and my interlocutor told
me that he believed *no* college now brewed within its walls. After
the defeat, I thought of the stages of the Decline and Fall of

the only other college in which, from actual
recent experience, I can imagine the possibility of
the exorcism,

Strongbeerum! discede a lay-fratre Petro,

if lay-brother Peter were so silly as to abuse, or
play tricks with, the good gift.

I have never had many experiences of real
'home-brewed,' but two which I had were pleasing. There was much home-brewing in East
Anglia at the time I lived there, and I once got the
village carpenter to give me some of his own
manufacture. It was as good light ale as I ever
wish to drink (many times better than the
wretched stuff that Dora has foisted on us), and he
told me that, counting in every expense for
material, cost and wear of plant, etc., it came to
about a penny[1] a quart. The other was very

Things: and how a sad but noble ode might be written (by the
right man) on the Fates of Greek and Beer at Oxford. He would
probably refer in the first strophe to the close of the *Eumenides*; in
its antistrophe to Mr. Swinburne's great adaptation thereof in
regard to Carlyle and Newman; while the epode and any
reduplication of the parts would be occupied by showing how the
departing entities were of no equivocal magnificence like the
Eumenides themselves; of no flawed perfection (at least as it
seemed to their poet) like the two great English writers, but wholly
admirable and beneficent—too good for the generation who
would banish them, and whom they banished.

[1] This was one of the best illustrations of the old phrase, 'a good
pennyworth,' that I ever knew *for certain*. I add the two last words
because of a mysterious incident of my youth. I and one of my
sisters were sitting at a window in a certain seaside place when we
heard, both of us distinctly and repeatedly, this mystic street cry:
'A bible and a pillow-case for a penny!' I rushed downstairs to
secure this bargain, but the crier was now far off, and it was too
late.

different. The late Lord de Tabley—better or at least longer known as Mr. Leicester Warren—once gave a dinner at the Athenaeum at which I was present, and had up from his Cheshire cellars some of the old ale for which that county used to be famous, to make flip after dinner. It was shunned by most of the pusillanimous guests, but not by me, and it was excellent. But I should like to have tried it unflipped.[1]

I never drank mum, which all know from *The Antiquary*, some from 'The Ryme of Sir Lancelot Bogle,' and some again from the notice which Mr. Gladstone's love of Scott (may it plead for him!) gave it once in some Budget debate, I think. It is said to be brewed of wheat, which is not in its favour (wheat was meant to be eaten, not drunk), and very bitter, which is. Nearly all bitter drinks are good. The only time I ever drank 'spruce' beer I did not like it. The comeliest of black malts is, of course, that noble liquor called Guinness. Here at least I think England cannot match Ireland, for our stouts are, as a rule, too sweet and 'clammy.' But there used to be in the country districts a sort of light porter which was one of the most refreshing liquids conceivable for hot weather. I have drunk it in Yorkshire at the foot of Roseberry Topping, out of big stone bottles like

[1] By the way, are they still as good for flip at New College, Oxford, as they were in the days when it numbered hardly any undergraduates except scholars, and one scholar of my acquaintance had to himself a set of three rooms and a garden? And is 'The Island' at Kennington still famous for the same excellent compound?

champagne magnums. But that was nearly sixty years ago. Genuine lager beer is no more to be boycotted than genuine hock, though, by the way, the best that I ever drank (it was at the good town of King's Lynn) was Low not High Dutch in origin. It was so good that I wrote to the shippers at Rotterdam to see if I could get some sent to Leith, but the usual difficulties in establishing connection between wholesale dealers and individual buyers prevented this. It was, however, something of a consolation to read the delightful name, 'our top-and-bottom-fermentation beer,' in which the manufacturer's letter, in very sound English for the most part, spoke of it. *English* lager I must say I have never liked; perhaps I have been unlucky in my specimens. And good as Scotch strong beer is, I cannot say that the lighter and medium kinds are very good in Scotland. In fact, in Edinburgh I used to import beer of this kind from Lincolnshire,[1] where there is no mistake

---

[1] It came from Alford, the *chef-lieu*, if it cannot be called the capital, of the Tennyson country. I have pleasant associations with the place, quite independent of the beery ones. And it made me, partially at least, alter one of the ideas of my early criticism—that time spent on a poet's local habitations was rather wasted. I have always thought 'The Dying Swan' one of its author's greatest things, and one of the champion examples of pure poetry in English literature. But I never fully *heard* the "eddying song" that "flooded"

> the creeping mosses and clambering weeds,
> And the willow branches hoar and dank,
> And the wavy swell of the soughing reeds,
> And the wave-worn horns of the echoing bank,
> And the silvery marish-flowers that throng
> The desolate creeks and pools among—

till I *saw* them.

about it. My own private opinion is that John Barleycorn, north of Tweed, says: 'I am for whisky, and not for ale.'

'Cider and perry,' says Burton, 'are windy drinks'; yet he observes that the inhabitants of certain shires in England (he does not, I am sorry to say, mention Devon), of Normandy in France, and of Guipuzcoa in Spain, "are no whit offended by them." I have never liked perry on the few occasions on which I have tasted it; perhaps because its taste has always reminded me of the smell of some stuff that my nurse used to put on my hair when I was small. But I certainly have been no whit offended by cider, either in divers English shires, including very specially those which Burton does not include, Devon, Dorset, and Somerset, or in Normandy. The Guipuzcoan variety I have, unfortunately, had no opportunity of tasting. Besides, perry seems to me to be an abuse of that excellent creature the pear, whereas cider-apples furnish one of the most cogent arguments to prove that Providence had the production of alcoholic liquors directly in its eye. They are good for nothing else whatever, and they are excellent good for that. I think I like the weak ciders, such as those of the west and of Normandy, better than the stronger ones,[1] and draught cider much better than bottled. That of Norfolk, which has been much commended of late, I have never tasted; but I have had both Western and West-Midland cider in my cellar,

[1] Herefordshire and Worcestershire cider can be very strong, and the perry, they say, still stronger.

often in bottle and once or twice in cask. It is a pity that the liquor—extremely agreeable to the taste, one of the most thirst-quenching to be anywhere found, of no over-powering alcoholic strength as a rule, and almost sovereign for gout—is not to be drunk without caution, and sometimes has to be given up altogether from other medical aspects. Qualified with brandy—a mixture which was first imparted to me at a roadside inn by a very amiable Dorsetshire farmer whom I met while walking from Sherborne to Blandford in my first Oxford 'long'—it is capital: and cider-cup (*v. inf.*) who knoweth not? If there be any such, let him not wait longer than to-morrow before establishing knowledge, though we may say more of it here. As for the pure juice of the apple, four gallons a day per man used to be the harvest allowance in Somerset when I was a boy. It is refreshing only to think of it now.

Of mead or metheglin, the third indigenous liquor of Southern Britain, I know little. Indeed, I should have known nothing at all of it had it not been that the parish-clerk and sexton of the Cambridgeshire village where I lived, and the caretaker of a vinery which I rented, was a bee-keeper and mead-maker. He gave me some once. I did not care much for it. It was like a sweet weak beer, with, of course, the special honey flavour. But I should imagine that it was susceptible of a great many different modes of preparation, and it is obvious, considering what it is made of, that it could be brewed of almost any strength. Old literary notices generally speak of it as strong.

CHAPTER XI

'MIXED LIQUORS'

WHAT did Charles Lamb mean, in those 'Confessions of a Drunkard,' which oscillate in a rather ghastly manner between truth and fiction, irony and sincerity, art and nature, by 'those juggling compositions which under the name of "mixed liquors" conceal a good deal of brandy, etc.?' He cannot have meant punch, for he has already mentioned it separately. The phrase, with what follows, is hardly applicable to 'bishop' and its class, or to 'cups,' but it must apparently mean something of one sort or another like these. At any rate, though things of the kind, except 'Swedish punch' and one or two others, seldom occur in a cellar-book, they certainly cannot be made without things that do occur there; so it may not be improper to include here something about them, since they are 'mixed liquors' in a special and, one would hope from Lamb's description of their namesakes, less deleterious sense.

Bishop itself would, from books, appear to have

been in former days very specially an Oxford drink, but it certainly was not common there in my time. In fact, on the only occasion on which I did see and taste it, I made it myself in my own rooms, for joint consumption with a friend (not Creighton), who, as a matter of fact, actually did become a bishop later. It is, as I have found more people not know than know in this ghastly thin-faced time of ours, simply mulled port. You take a bottle of that noble liquor and put it in a saucepan, adding as much or as little water as you can reconcile to your taste and conscience, an orange cut in half (I believe some people squeeze it slightly), and plenty of cloves (you may stick them in the orange if you have a mind). Sugar or no sugar at discretion, and with regard to the character of the wine. Put it on the fire, and as soon as it is warm, and begins to steam, light it. The flames will be of an imposingly infernal colour, quite different from the light blue flicker of spirits or of claret mulled. Before it has burned too long pour it into a bowl, and drink it as hot as you like. It is an excellent liquor, and I have found it quite popular with ladies. I think it is said (but I have not the book at hand) to have played the mischief with Alaric Tudor, the sorriest, though not the most disagreeable, of *The Three Clerks*; but then it was made of public-house port, which was probably half elder wine and half potato spirit.

Of its titular superiors, 'Cardinal' and 'Pope,' the former is only a rather silly name for mulled claret, while 'Pope,' *i.e.* mulled burgundy, is Anti-christian, from no mere Protestant point of view. *No* burgundy is really suitable for mulling, while to mull good burgundy is a capital crime. It is quite different with *vin brûlé*, a very popular beverage in Old France, and a regular Christmas and New Year tradition in the Channel Islands. When made of an unpretentious Bordeaux, it wants no dilution, of course, and if it is fairly stout wine, should want no fortifying. Some sugar it will certainly want, not to correct acidity, but to fill out body and flavour; a cloved and cloven lemon instead of the orange of bishop, a saucepan, a fire, and goblets. It will flame with less ghastly gorgeousness than the stronger liquor, but prettily enough, and it is exceedingly grateful and comforting. Indeed, virtues which it is not lawful to mention are attributed to it in Old French literature of the Pantagruelist variety.

Was there any negus in the length and breadth of the land during the recent revival of Christmas festivities? A hundred years ago, as everybody who reads knows, it was omnipresent both at public entertainments (where it may be suspected that few landlords were as 'liberal' as Mr. Jingle accused him of Rochester of being when he was presented with Dr. Slammer's card) and privately in houses before the bed-candles were taken. Even after dinner (*vide* Scott in *St. Ronan's Well* and the self-thoughtfulness of Mr. Winter-blossom) it seems to have held up its head with neat wine and punch. In my own time, and only in the earlier part of that, I remember it at children's parties. Port negus is not bad, and is indeed a poor relation of bishop; but one would hardly take it except as a kind of emergency drink after being kept out late in snow or rain, after a long railway journey in an unwarmed carriage, or the like. Modern sherries of the drier and less full-bodied kind make negus impossible; with a full golden or brown you may make a fair alternative to the port mixture. Hot water ('screeching hot, ye divil') and sugar are the properties of the compound, lemon-slices, etc., its accidents. I have never been quite sure whether the 'wine and water' so frequently mentioned of old, and in fact regarded as a sort of necessary ladies' nightcap, was negus, or merely cold 'grog' of wine. Our ancestors, I regret to say, had rather a habit of putting water into wine—a proceeding partly connected with, and perhaps also partly explaining, their long sittings.

Flip and punch having been spoken of else-where, we may pass from winter to summer drinks, only premising that some of the bottled punches formerly obtainable were very deadly. I remember partaking of a bowl made from one such in Scilly, *anno* 1867, with a very agreeable, and soon to be hospitable officer of Her Majesty's 20th Regiment and an old Oxford parson, both of whom were the best of company. The basis of the compound seemed to be arrack, and it was by no means unpalatable. But hardly ever, I think, in all my life have I been so feelingly appreciative of the Vauxhall 'next morning' before spoken of, or of that experienced by Mr. Tudor at the other end of Cornwall.

Cups, unless made of shocking stuff, or treacherously strong, involve no such punishment, and they are notoriously sometimes constructed in such a fashion as to be little stronger than, if as strong as, 'temperance drinks.' On the other hand, they can be raised to much higher powers. I once invented one which was extremely popular, and had a curious history later. Instead of soda water I used sparkling Moselle, in the proportion of a pint of this to a bottle of claret, with thick slices of pine-apple instead of lemon, and one lump of ice as big as a baby's head.[1] It was astonishing how the people lapped it up, and nobody complained next day (I gave it at an

[1] I think this mixture may be triumphantly vindicated against any charge of 'confusion,' such as may be brought against others, especially the once celebrated 'Bismarck.' Between the flavours of stout and of champagne there is no possible *liaison*. The former simply overwhelms the latter; and all the wine does is to make the beer more intoxicating and more costly. Thus the thing is at once vicious and vulgar. But the delicate flowery tastes and bouquets of the claret and the moselle make, in another sense, a real 'bouquet,' and the sparkle of the one wine gives just what the other has not. The advice about the 'baby's head' may seem to run contrary not merely to that usually given in wine-catalogues and store-lists— 'Do not put ice *in* cups,' but also to my own remarks on icing claret and champagne. But I think there is a distinction. First, the 'neat' flavour of the wine is, in cups, already submerged by the mixture of sugar, spirit, cucumber, borage and what not, and so is tolerably proof against mere contact with ice. Secondly, the progressive dilution by the melting ice does no harm, unless the more generous elements of the compound have been *very* stingily proportioned, which in this instance is certainly not the case. Thirdly, the floating iceberg rejoices the sight and, if it bobs against them, the lips, especially if the container is one of those brown-and-yellow, straight-sided, three-handled 'toby'-ware vessels which are cups' best (temporary) home.

evening party) of headache, though some ladies did say: 'Wasn't that delicious cup of yours *rather* strong? I slept *so* soundly after it!' But that is not the history. Some years after I had invented it I gave the receipt in an article in the *Saturday Review*, which used at that time to confide to me most books on eating and drinking. Before long it began to appear in such books themselves, as indeed I had altruistically expected, for they are almost inevitably compilations. But the gradation of titles was very amusing. The first borrower honestly quoted it as 'Saturday Review Cup'; the second simply headed it 'Another Cup.' But the third trumped both of them *and* me, for with a noble audacity he (or *she*, as I think it was) called it 'My Own Cup.'

Receipts for claret-cup are innumerable. Everybody has tasted it when it appeared to be composed of nothing but a little bad *ordinaire* and a great deal of soda water: and from this, in both Latin and English senses, 'vile' mixture you may ascend to the most complicated prescriptions with sherry, brandy, liqueurs of various sorts, lemon, cucumber, borage (which always should be there, if possible), and half a dozen other things.

Champagne- and moselle-cups seem to me to come under the double sentence more than once applied in these pages. If they are made of good wine they are wicked; if of bad, unpardonable. Indeed, on the whole, it seems to me that no cup comes up to cider-cup, for the simple reason that there you are not contaminating but corroborating. A very little fizzing water, a good dose of stout well-flavoured sherry, just a *pousse* of brandy, with lemon and borage, will make *the* drink for hot weather, and the drinker will escape some inconveniences formerly hinted at as attending the drinking of 'apple wine' neat.

Porter-cup and beer-cup I have only heard of, and do not much fancy, though of normally strong Bass and a little soda water I can say: '*Bu et approuvé*,' as in certain circumstances superior to bottled Bass itself.

In looking over this chapter I notice that I have said nothing here (nor anything earlier except in the case of true, that is to say beer-made, 'flip') of mixtures with milk and eggs. For the milk-class I have no great affection. 'Rum and milk' has been often celebrated in the words of Mercury, and sometimes in the songs of Apollo; but I do not think the rum is improved. Whisky and milk is rather better, especially if the whisky is very 'smoky,' for this corrects the mawkishness of the milk. I remember some, partaken of on a solitary walk in more than usually (for it was very early in the year) solitary Skye, from Uig by the Quiraing to Stenscholl. It seemed a thing in place, though the dispenser was a young person quite unbeautiful, extremely unkempt, and with no apparent knowledge of English beyond the name of the required mixture; and though the beach afterwards afforded neither golden cricket-ball nor coin-filled casket from the wreck of the *Carmilhan*. Brandy goes with milk even worse than rum; I never tried gin. As for 'pullet-sperm in the brewage' once more, sherry-and-egg and brandy-

and-egg ('cock-a-doodle broth') are well-known restoratives; and some have recommended a sort of prairie oyster, made by breaking a raw egg into a half-tumbler of rough red wine of claret type, and swallowing it without beating. But I cannot reconcile myself to the port and beaten-up egg which mountaineering books occasionally prescribe. The two flavours appear to me to 'swear at' each other as trucelessly as do certain colours.[1]

With all these mixed drinks, however, and the more so with them the more mixed they are, there is perhaps, in the purged considerate mind of age, a doubt whether they are not vanities. Punch escapes by virtue of its numerous venerable and amiable associations, and, to speak frankly, of its undeniable charms; and at the other end cider cup, for the last reason, if not for the others. Bishop and *vin brûlé* diffuse an agreeable warmth, and so on and so on. (By the way 'burnt sherry,' though it has at least one great testimonial from Dickens, is not directly known to and is rather doubted by me, while *Hunted Down*, the same great writer's and good drinker's commemoration of burnt brandy, certainly does not favour it.) But they are all very liable to lead to the consumption of too much sugar, and sugar is as unwholesome to the possibly unscientific but practically experienced judgment as its derivative

---

[1] For 'purl' see note on 'Artemisias' in the chapter on 'Liqueurs.' Theoretically, I believe it should be warmed with a red-hot poker: but the only experiment of the kind I ever made was far from successful.

alcohol is healthful.[1] They all slightly suggest that mystical (but, the longer you live and the more you think, more profoundly justified) biblical curse on 'confusion.' Spirit asks for water (which thing is an allegory), but wine and beer ask for nothing but their own goodly selves, and somebody to drink, appreciate, and not abuse them. There was, as usual, an infinitely wider scope and range of action than that directly implied in the great sentence twice quoted in part already, '*Simple of itself*; I'll no pullet-sperm in my brewage.' And yet I do not recant my exaltation of flip and some others, or my recipe for 'Cup.' One must be inconsistent sometimes.

---

[1] I had rather have the brewing and distilling done outside my body, instead of inside, as is the way of the abstainers.

CHAPTER XII

BOTTLES AND GLASSES

SOMETHING was said, in the opening chapter of
this booklet, of certain special wine-glasses; and
there has been mention of bottles—the con-
tainers, not merely the units contained—now
and then. But there should, I think, be a little
more on both points before we conclude. Bottles
are extremely interesting things; and as for glasses
and decanters, they can be delightful works of
pure art. Without the former the bins of a cellar
are as the walls of Balclutha, desolate; and there
should in every cellar be a shelf of glasses, ready
for the owner's private experiments or for his
public liberality. One of my pleasantest cellar
remembrances is that of dispensing at the door-
way a glass of pure Clyne Lish (I think it was) to
an oyster-wife who used to supply us with excellent natives at one and ninepence a dozen. 'You
won't want any water?' said I, and the lady
ejaculated 'Na! Na!' with a smile worthy of
Ocean itself.

I do not know when the standard bottle or 'reputed' quart actually existing—one-sixth of a gallon or rather over twenty-six ounces—was evolved. But everybody knows that pints and quarts themselves were, till lately, very 'movable' feast-companions. Not to mention the ancient Scots pint, which was two English quarts, there still is, for chemical use, the 'Winchester quart,' which is five pints and is a stately vessel. I never saw wine bottled in it, but I have often used it as a receiver for spirits drawn from the cask. The gradations of the standard bottle—its multiples and fractions—are, as generally accepted, the rehoboam, or imperial, 8 bots.; the jeroboam, 6; the double magnum, 4; the tappit hen, 3; the magnum, 2; the bottle itself; the imperial pint; the reputed pint; and the quarter-bottle, some-times called 'nip,' 'baby,' and other pet names.[1] They look very pretty 'all of a row,' especially in champagne form, from double magnum to 'baby': and once, when I found that a child of mine had adopted an empty set for playthings, I would, had I been a person of property, have done as Boswell did or meant to do for his Veronica, when he added to her portion because of her attention to his idol.[2]

[1] I decline to admit the 'imperial *half*-pint' in which beer is sometimes confined. Some readers may remember Christopher North's fine indignation at Sir H. Davy's 'half-a-pint per man is *not too much!*' But this was at any rate *wine*. *I* once heard a human creature say cheerfully that one of these wretched apologies contained just *beer* enough 'for him *and his wife!*'

[2] It is a pity that the practice of 'lozenging' bottles, with date of vintage, initials of possessor, name of house, etc., etc., has (except

I am not sure that I ever possessed, or even that I ever saw, an 'imperial,' but I have had several jeroboams, which used to be not uncommon vessels with Scotch merchants for dispensing single gallons of whisky. They retained more of the portliness of the older wine-bottle than is now customary, that bottle having of late elongated and 'slimmed' its proportions. In the earliest nineteenth century (and one has come across examples even later) there was a tendency to widen and almost 'flange' the bottom. This made the vessel stand more firmly and held the crust better: but it would have been very awkward to bin without the then usual bed of sawdust. I think this sawdust was rather a mistake. It may have, when quite dry, kept the wine at an even temperature and prevented breakages, besides giving an air of age when brought up. But it encouraged insects and fungi in the corks; and in case of leakage it made a most disastrous hotbed, which sometimes quite spoilt the wine.

Such flanged bottles had some merits in picturesqueness and individuality. Earlier still the popular form seems to have been not cylindrical but globular, or like the *bocksbeutel* flasks of Steinwein. There are at Oxford some very attrac-

---

perhaps in the cellars of some private persons who possess the not universal combination of money and sense) apparently gone out. For it gives the individuality, more or less, which is a great secret of enjoyment.At the same time I am bound to say that my own (I think single) experience of it was not lucky. It was in the case of some '87 Lafite, which was lozenged when I bought it; and which never justified the distinction.

tive examples of the round shape rescued from ignominious burial and enshrined in the library of All Souls College. In fact, of old days there must have been a variety of form, which still lingers in liqueur-vessels to some extent. Of those which have survived, the red-brown hock and green moselle bottles, with their tapering outline, are the most graceful. At the Palatine Restaurant in Manchester they formerly used hock bottles as water-carafes. As for the 'kicked' bottom of so many French wine and brandy bottles, it is perhaps, to the eye, preferable to a flat one: but of course it makes fraud easier. If I do not mistake, it is but a few years since a French Minister of Commerce addressed a vigorous allocution to his countrymen on the subject. And I know that in measuring a bottle of brandy bottled in France against one bottled in England I have sometimes found the 'kick' responsible for a deficiency of nearly a sherry-glassful in the former.[1]

With decanters—those half-way houses between bottle and glass—one comes to questions of pure art. They can be very lovely things indeed; they can be frightfully ugly; and it is possible to

---

[1] In bidding adieu to 'bottles' one glance may be pardoned at the former position of the *pint*. Not only does John Thorpe count his and his friends' consumption of port by pints, and several pints, but, later, Mr. Pickwick 'finishes his *second* pint of particular port'—evidently a regular function. Why not a bottle? A little later still Will Waterproof had *a* pint—though, one suspects, again without prejudice to another. At any rate, the performance had no 'stint' in it. Yet the wine is better in the larger vessel, and there is less relative danger and loss from crust.

have them without any great outlay—or was possible when it was possible to have anything without a great outlay—good to look at and good to use. Body-colour, when they are not kept pure white, should be, I think, restricted to a pale green—the shade of a moselle flask. Blues and reds kill the natural hues of wine, though a not too deep yellow is permissible. The noblest decanter I ever possessed was one I saw stuck away on a high shelf at Powells' (whose departure, by the way, from Whitefriars is sad). It had been made to order for the contents of a 'tappit-hen' (*v. sup.*), but rejected by the (saving his reverence) idiotic orderer, and I bought it. It was of the flattened cone shape, white, fluted, and with a little frill round its fair throat. Unfortunately I never could get an actual tappit hen of claret to put in it— they were not infrequent at the sale of old Scotch cellars thirty or forty years ago, but are very rare now. However, it contented itself with a magnum cheerfully enough: and I am not sure that the bouquet did not develop better for the empty space. (I need hardly say that to decant more than one bottle into the same vessel is a very risky experiment.) At any rate it used to look imposing under a seven-light brass candlestick which Mr. Benson made for me. The same admirable craftsmen, who, like all persons deserving that noun and adjective, would take just as much trouble for you if you gave them a half-guinea order as if it had been such as one of their commissions I once saw on its way to Russia—a cut-glass service worth fifteen hundred pounds—made me a set of claret jugs, two of each size—pint, bottle, and magnum—of the pilgrim bottle shape, green, fluted, but with rounded bottoms, not flat like the 'hen-master.' And from them, from Salviati's, and from other sources one picked up things not unworthy of their intended contents.

The one drawback of cut-glass decanters— besides their cost, but apart from the purpose recommended by Count Considine in *Charles O'Malley*—is their great weight. The beauty of them no one can well contest; though I think the material shews better in the wine-glass than in the decanter. Few kinds shew off the wine itself better than the so-called 'Black Forest' type, which separates a top and a bottom mass of liquid by four slender tube-columns. My earliest recollection of it (I do not think it was at all common before the middle of the nineteenth century) was derived from mounted examples in the window of a silversmith named Sachs, who used to have a shop—the only one in a highly genteel neighbourhood—below Connaught Square, and close to that quaint chapel and burying-ground which, according to legend, saw the 'resurrecting' of Sterne's body. This was as far back as the early fifties. Afterwards they multiplied, and were even sold with whisky and other things in them, so that they have become quite common. But that matters little. Of more elaborate forms, curly snaky things, circlets with a big hole in the middle and the like, I am not sure. Simplicity is a mighty Goddess in the flagon, which should aim at displaying not so much itself as the wine.

It is otherwise with the wine-*glass* for not a few reasons, one of the chief being that you naturally hold it up, and look at it, and play with it in your hands. It should never in the least obscure the colour of the wine, or the possibility of looking through that wine itself and both sides of the glass to the light—a point in which some of the more gaudy Venetian examples seem to me faulty. But short of this, the taste and fancy of the designer and the glass-worker may find very wide exercise. Here cut glass—a bevel and rim of *un*-cut being kept for the lip—is in some respects, for those who can stand its cost, the best of all. It is heavy, but not, on this scale, too heavy; while its very weight keeps it steady, and saves it from the exertions of any but the strongest handmaid.

It is true that there is nothing that some servants will not break. The *mousseline* glasses, of which in their early days Thackeray complained that they 'were not only enormous, but broke by dozens,' fly like chaff before them; and with the aid of the pantry tap (most handy for such a purpose) almost anything can be broken. They sometimes display a really uncanny acquaintance with the secrets of natural philosophy. I had a parlour-maid once who was evidently well up in the doctrine of transmission of forces. She arranged three decanters, partly full of wine, back to back and touching each other, on the shelf of a buffet-cupboard, so that the outermost just projected a quarter of an inch in front of the edge. The shutting of the door, even quite gently, necessarily caused, as will be seen, the destruction of all three; the door itself breaking No. 1, that cracking No. 2, and that in turn accomplishing the ruin of No. 3. It was a beautiful demonstration in physics, but I wish it had occurred somewhere else. In fact, the loss of glass is so enormous that I once made a sober calculation showing how at the time—some thirty years ago when silver was cheap—it would have paid to lay in a moderate but sufficient service in pure argent. But unfortunately glass—at least so it seems to me—is your only ware for wine. I never literally put in practice the famous Welsh saying, *Gwin o eur*— 'wine from *gold*.' But silver, though excellent for beer (even there it is not so good as pewter), has never pleased me for wine.

Of the shapes and sizes of glasses there were no end, if one spoke at all fully. It may be said generally that those with a swelling lip are bad; those with a pinched-in one good, especially for wines of much bouquet. 'Brimmers' and 'bumpers' are jovial and time-honoured, but better sung about than indulged in. And if our fathers meant by 'No heel-taps' that you were always to drink the whole glassful at once, even with allowance of 'skylight,' I think that, for once, our fathers were wrong. Beverage wines may be drunk in that fashion, of course, but nothing choice, and very specially not port, good claret or burgundy. But I prefer to think that they only barred the keeping of a remnant when you filled, so that you did not 'drink fair.'

Beyond all doubt there is a certain pre-established harmony between different wines and different shapes, sizes and even colours of glasses. Claret never tastes well in a small glass; burgundy I think even worse. Port is more tolerant. The old green hock-glasses were suitable enough for the wine they were named from; but I always thought that it, and all other light white wines, tasted best in some faint straw-coloured, bell-shaped things on very tall stems, which a friend was kind enough to bring me straight from Nuremberg. I have spoken before of the Salviati cloud-white, avanturine, and blue for French red wines. They did not so well suit port—which goes best in cut glass—or any white wine. Sherry being always the most accommodating of liquors, you may drink it in glasses small or large, white or coloured, plain or fancy in shape. If it is good it will always be good in any; and if it is bad, none will save it.[1]

As for champagne, there is room for real controversy about that. Its vehicles to the mouth may be classed fourfold: the old tall 'flutes,' the modern ballet-girl-skirt inverted, which is supposed to have been one of the marks of the viciousness of the French Second Empire, but which all the world hastened to adopt; tumblers; and a nondescript group of large glasses, varying from claret to goblet shape, and sometimes

[1] What has been admitted to be a sort of 'sin' in liqueurs has a 'solace,' as Milton would say, in the opening they give for various and pretty glasses. For most kinds there is nothing better than white glass with gold-leaf arabesques or flowers. Green chartreuse and green curaçao, as well the red liquids, ask for plain white in colour, but with shape and cutting at discretion. Nor are the tiny crumpled Venetian tumblers to be objected to.

enormous in size. Of these I bar, at once and without appeal, the tumbler. I do this regretfully, for many good men have given me much good wine in it; but I think it is WRONG. In the first place, the wine never tastes quite right out of tumblers: they demoralise it, and approximate Reims to Saumur. And in the second, there is no stem for the finger-tips to play with; now a wine-glass without a stem is as bad as some other 'creations' without a waist—or a neck, for after all the sacque, which has no waist, is a creation of some merit.

The fault of the miscellaneous glasses, some of which, however, are not bad, is that they are not *distinctive* enough. A wine of such unique charac-ter as champagne—for after all other sparkling wines are pale copies and corrupt followings of Dom Pérignon's great discovery—ought to have a glass to itself, peculiar in something besides mere size. This connection both the flutes and the inverted skirts duly meet: and I have never entirely or decisively made up my mind between them, using now one now the other 'while it was day.' I have always been willing to recognise an overruling Providence in the affairs of this world—a Providence which makes the punish-ment fit the crime (the thirst of the Pussyfoots in the Sixth Circle, *if they are allowed there*, will be ten times that of the drunkards) and adjusts the supply to the demand. And so I have sometimes thought that the flute is most suitable to sweet champagnes, and the other to dry. The former must not be too small, a fault perhaps not unknown in the days when a single bottle of champagne was made to do for a dozen people. The latter should not be too large, or you get a clumsy something more like a *tazza* or a fruit 'comport' than a glass. Its most practical form is undoubtedly that in which the stem is pierced nearly to the foot with a thin tube, for this maintains the sparkle remarkably. On the other hand the glass has to be very heavy, and it is rather difficult to keep the shaft of the funnel quite clean. But such a glass, filled with *œil-de-perdrix* wine, the bubbles lazily ascending through the stem and diffusing themselves fountain-fashion through the upper liquor, is a beautiful sight— promising a pleasant satisfaction to other senses, and good to close a chapter with, even if one perceives no immediate chance of seeing it again. *Fuit* and *fuimus*—I take leave to repeat the burden of my book in various forms—are not always mournful words to the wiser and not too pusillanimous mind.

CHAPTER XIII

CELLAR ARRANGEMENTS

IT may seem rather absurd for a man whose
command of cellar-room, and his opportunity for
availing himself of it, have always been extremely
limited, to write a chapter under this heading.
But the book, small as it is, and so suiting its
circumstances, would hardly be complete without such a chapter. And this is more especially the
case because the genesis of the Cellar-Book itself
was connected with the fact that once and once
only, a cellar such as it was, small but fairly
perfect, 'did,' like the sword and pistol of the
heroine of 'Billy Taylor,' 'come at my command.'

Until I was nearly forty such liquids as I
possessed had to endure very inferior accommodation. Up to the time of the close of the first
third of the nineteenth century, I have reason to
believe that London middle-class houses, as indeed others were and continued to be in the
country, were not so ill provided in this respect.
Port, which everybody who had even a few

hundreds a year drank, and of which an ordinary family would consume its bottle often, if not daily, was, as has been pointed out earlier, quite cheap; and though few people who were not positively well to do might lay down whole pieces for future consumption, it was probably bought in good quantity for more or less immediate drinking. But as this habit fell off, and as houses began to be built, cheaply and without thought but in immense numbers, all round London, the cellar lost its importance. The house, at Southampton, which I first knew, and which was, I suppose, built early in the nineteenth century, had, if I am not mistaken, a good one. But those in London just north of Kensington Gardens, where I passed most of my life between five years old and twenty-three, had, I think, nothing but a cupboard under the kitchen stairs—an arrangement which secured (not to mention the proximity, not immediate but too close, of the kitchen fire) constant shaking from trampling of servants up and down. Nor were things much better in others where I kept house independently later, as far as Guernsey and London were concerned, though in Elgin, where my abode was a *ci-devant* hotel converted into a school-house, Bacchus was better accommodated.

In the early eighties, however, I moved into one of the new regions west of Kensington, and took, somewhat rashly, a 7-14-21 years' lease of a house never previously occupied, indeed not quite ready for occupation, and the first of its pretty long row of neighbours to be inhabited. As in such cases I believe is not (or was not) uncommon, the builders were extremely liberal in decoration and internal arrangement, the house, while in process of completion, serving as a sort of advertisement to the rest of the row. They let me choose my papers; they furnished me with a bath of extraordinary elaborateness, where you could float on an upward douche like a cork in one of the shop-fountains, subject yourself to what was called a 'wave' (it was more ingenious than exhilarating), and by turning various cocks and levers in the hood, administer showers of most interesting variety. But what was even more to my taste was that they let me adjust, and charged me nothing for adjusting, an apartment in the basement which had, I think, been meant for a larder, to the purposes not of eating but of drink. It was not entirely subterranean, as the garden on which its window opened was much lower than the road; but its greatest length backed on solid earth, and there were no pipes or stoves too near. I never found it very much above or below the sacred 50°–55°. As for room, I had it spaced into 25 stone bins, 15 on one side and 10 on the other, graded, so that, without their being very deep, the lowest accommodated from 12 to 15 dozen, and the uppermost perhaps three. Unless you have large quantities of single wines, deep bins are a nuisance.

This, though no Domdaniel, seemed sufficiently like a real cellar to deserve a cellar-book, and accordingly that which forms the text of the present notes was started. But Fate is notoriously capricious, and though I am happy to say that the grim Eastern proverb as to Who 'comes in at the window when the house is finished' was not fulfilled, I was only allowed a very short possession. Scarely four times[1] had one of the big bins been filled and re-filled with light claret, as formerly mentioned, when I had to move my household into the country for the health's sake of one of its members, and content myself with chambers in town for the working days of the week. *There* a cupboard and an iron wine-bin sufficed; in the two country houses which I successively occupied there were cellars, but rather small ones, and I left off keeping the book regularly.

My cellar near Cambridge had one awkward peculiarity. It was approached through another of slightly lower level, and this outer cellar, at certain times of the year, used to be filled about a foot deep with the most pellucid water, apparently rising from the earth. This remained some time, and disappeared as it came. While it was there it necessitated the erection of a plank bridge to get to the wine, and incidentally made the house above rather damp. So a kind friend proposed to pump it out, and actually brought a garden-engine for the purpose. I had, while expressing due gratitude, to point out to him that in that case we should be pumping against the springs of half Cambridgeshire and an unknown

[1] Let me in gratitude name the fillers, Messrs. Harvey's 'Red Seal' Medoc, and Châteaux Bonneval, Laujac and Citran.

proportion of Essex and Suffolk, so that on the general principle of water finding its level, the operation would take some time, and it might be difficult to know what to do with what we pumped. I believe new water-works, for Cambridge itself, have since accomplished this piece of engineering more satisfactorily. Had I been longer there the damp would, no doubt, have worked wreckage. The butler at a house in Hampshire, which, though situated high up, must have had springs near it, told me that it was there hardly safe to leave wine, without actual recorking, for more than seven years. But in this instance I had small supplies, and moved in half that time, so no harm was done.

When, in 1895, I moved once more from another place in the south of England to Edinburgh, I inhabited, for the first four years, a large house somewhat to the west of the city, and dating from the early eighteenth century. Cellars of such houses in Scotland are generally ample; I know one in which even Mr. Crotchet's 'thousand dozen of wine' could be accommodated with the greatest ease, and leave room for at least another thousand, with casks to match. But though my abode had a large cellarage, it had evidently not—recently at least—been much used for the noblest purpose of such structures. There was an enormous coal-cellar, which one could and of course did—in the good days when colliers, *pace* Mr. Smillie, were quite happy with their moderate wages, and when coal merchants charged no more than twelve shillings a ton in summer—

fill for a whole year's consumption on the rather extravagant Northern scale. There was an intermediate apartment, hardly at all binned, but where you could put cases, casks, and iron wine bins if you chose. And then there was the innermost recess, which was prepared—after a fashion but not very amply—for wine storage.

It was greatly infested with rats, and for a time I was puzzled by having to add thermometers to the already considerable list of rat-foods. But before very long I found out the mystery. In looking to see that the cellar was not too cold (there was not much danger of its being too hot) one sloped the candle towards the instrument, and the grease dropped on the wood. It hung just above the top of an iron wine bin, and the ingenious beasts evidently climbed up without displacing the bottles. They, to do them justice, never lost me a drop that way, though they seem to have had designs, for we once discovered a sherry glass half-way down a rat hole. But their enemy, my Scotch terrier Bounce (whose pedigree I used to keep in the same drawer with my commission as Regius Professor) was more clumsy. He followed me one day without my knowledge, saw a rat, dashed at the bin, and I immediately found him yelling with fear and struggling with the *débris* and froth of two magnums of champagne. If he had got the rat it would have been some consolation for a rather expensive kind of sport.

The last stage, the longest, and (till it ended as all things end) the most abundantly furnished in wine, was not quite so abundantly furnished with room. The cellar of my house in Edinburgh itself was not so commodious as that which I organised in London, and it was partly under stairs. But since Craig-Leith stone does not transmit vibration as deal planks do, the resting place was steady enough. It was never too cold (I was able to meet that danger by a gas-jet put low down, for one at the usual height will simply mull your top-bins), and only in the hottest Septembers (which are Edinburgh's hottest months) did it verge on undue heat. It consisted of four very large and deep stone bins on the right as you entered, and of a narrow but longer angle-piece admitting some twenty small wooden partitions, one bottle deep, on one side, and a stool and shelf for jars, etc., on the other. There was also room for an iron champagne bin at one end, and a small decanting table with shelves beneath at the other. The great and rich might have scorned it; and their butlers certainly would. But by taking advantage of corners, etc., I found it capable of accommodating all the wine I wanted, in a fashion more conveniently accessible than far more stately magazines could boast. The deep bins I utilized at the back for storing wines too young to drink, and in front as homes for the small store-casks above spoken of; while the number of the shallow ones, which would hold three or four dozen apiece, admitted of separating different liquids so as to be got at at once.

Well! a cellar is an interesting place to fill, to contemplate when filled, and to empty in the

proper way. Nor, if you have to part with it, is its
memory other than agreeable. The doctrine of *ut
conviva satur* will not always hold; but it will here.[1]

---

[1] A talk of cellars would hardly seem complete without something
about that plague of the cellar-owner, 'corking.' I am happy to say
that I do not, as such, know very much about it. I remember being
told by a famous Fellow of a more famous College, at which I was
dining, that they had at one time been tried in this way to an
alarming extent, without being able to determine whether it was
the fault of the corks (I thought of Warton's

> Rode for a stomach, and inspected
> At annual bottlings, corks selected)

or that of the butler, or something like the biblical plague of
house-leprosy in the cellar itself. None of my cellar*ets*, for they were
little more, was thus cursed. Certainly I have seen, but only in the
case of some bottles bought at sales, corks in a quite Gehazi-like
condition from tip to wax. Such cases are no doubt hopeless. In
milder ones the wine may sometimes be made not undrinkable by
standing the decanter (which should have been specially bright
and dry) with the stopper out before a fire (but of course not too
near) for a time, which the restoration of the bouquet, if it *be*
restorable, will show. It should perhaps be said that this fungus-
growth, or whatever it is, which attacks other wines, does not seem
to be responsible for that so-called 'corking' of champagne, in
reference to which there is a sharp division between two races of
wine-merchants. The one protests, truly enough, that he can't
help it; but if you send back the peccant bottle he will give you a
fresh one. The other simply observes that he sends the cases as he
receives them, and has no more to do with it. The worst nuisance of
this corking is that a single bottle at a dinner-party will, by the filling
up of half-empty glasses, infect a much larger quantity of wine. It
gave me, however, once, an amusing moment. A physician of
distinction, who had made himself rather conspicuous by frequent
tirades in print against alcohol, positively disturbed his neighbours
at a public dinner by outcries against the corking of some, as it
seemed to me, quite innocent champagne. It may perhaps be well
to warn 'absent-minded beggars' that the 'cure by heat' above
suggested is *not* intended to be applied to the liquid, of which
Panard sang pleasantly, 'De ce vin gris Que je chéris L'écume!'
(Besides the information about Artemisias, I owe my friend Sir W.

T. Thiselton-Dyer the name of the 'corked wine' fungus, *Merulius lacrymans*, which is much too lovely to leave out, though it reached me a little late for the text. I hope that it will suggest to others, as it did to me, the famous 'Il en rougit, le traître!' with *pleure* instead of *rougit!*)

CONCLUSIO AD DIVERSOS

(WITH A FEW BARMECIDE INVITATIONS)

THE excuse for a proem to these few pages may seem to want repetition and emphasising in the case of a 'Post-face'; but it is perhaps not a mere paradox to say that the smaller the book the greater the need for such a thing. Among the various groups to whom an *Envoi* may not be superfluous I shall not omit, though I recognise the almost hopelessness of their admission, the Prohibitionists, open and concealed. It would, I fear, be utterly useless to content oneself with the good-humoured request of Dorat to the French *philosophes*:

> Mais, pour Dieu, soyez bonnes gens,
> Et, si vous pouvez, plus modestes!

For if there were any possibility of their being *bonnes gens*, they could hardly be what they are.

In my journalist days I was once complimented by an editor on possessing an unusual variety of 'jackets'; literary, political, historical, philosophical, culinary, and even theological, not to mention others. In donning the theological one I had not neglected (nor I hope in the other cases) to qualify myself to some extent for the wearing. I think few theologians will disagree with me when I say that thanklessness towards God and malice towards men constitute about as awkward a 'soul-*diathesis*' as can be imagined.[1] Nor, moving the calculus, will the preference of questionable 'scientific' theories to age-long practical experience come out much better. When the doctors and the Reverends (self-dubbed and other) and the occasional magistrates who cackle about the mischiefs of alcohol, condescend to face facts,[2] there may be something more to say to them. But no more at present, except to urge the most strenuous opposition to the subdolous and impertinent foreign interference which they are calling to their aid; and to express regret that Archbishops and Bishops, if they do not definitely set themselves against the advice of St. Paul and the

[1] Prohibitionists disclaim the 'malice,' of course. But so, with much more reason, would Torquemada have done. The 'thanklessness' speaks for itself.

[2] Here is one for which I have more than once vouched in print, and which I defy anyone to invalidate. Six years' experience (1868–1874) of the island of Guernsey, where you could get blind drunk for sixpence; a population of between 30,000 and 40,000; a garrison frequently renewed; sailors from many parts of the world dropping in; scarcely any police; *no* serious crime; hardly any minor disorder; and a splendid bill of health. When a man commits a crime under what is miscalled the 'influence' of drink, he should, where possible, be punished double —once for the bad act, and once for the misuse of the good thing, by forcing it to reveal his true nature.

practice of Christ, should join movements, the clear effect, and in some cases the hardly disguised object, of which is to make the adoption of that advice and the imitation of that practice impossible.

Turning to the sheep after leaving these goats (though I have always thought it a little hard on the goat, which is generally a good-looking and sometimes an agreeable animal) I have to apologise to greater experts than myself for any over-positiveness of statement and any deficiency of information. I am only an amateur, of course; only a man who has made the study and enjoyment of wine and its fellows (their kinds, their merits and their innumerable and world-ranging associations, in life and literature, in history and society) one of the amusements, relaxations, and auxiliaries of a rather unusually hard-working life.[1] As one looks back over

[1] I should not be dealing candidly with my reader, if I did not warn him that Pussyfoot scientists call the state of perceived well-being and capability for well-doing, which alcohol induces, 'toxic euphoria.' Toxic euphoria as a phrase is good; it is even better than 'mobled queen'; it is delicious. It brings a fresh pang at the approaching *dys*thanasia of its language which some people (including pretty surely the Pussyfoot scientists themselves) are trying to bring about. But as they use it, it carries a vain and fallacious meaning, fondly if not fraudulently invented. As real men of science (who cannot be too carefully distinguished from 'scientists') have pointed out before now, alcohol is auto-antidotic, its narcotic quality tending to dispel its other tendency, as Mr. Gargery so delicately put it, to 'over stim*i*late.' The toxicity, as all bad things unfortunately do not *yet* do, whatever Apocatastasis may bring about (if they want Greek they can have plenty) vanishes; the euphoria, as all good things do, and always will do, remains.

such a life there are many things that one regards with thankfulness. It is good to have walked by oneself five hundred miles in twenty days and one pair of boots (never needing the cobbler till the very last day) without any training and with a fairly heavy knapsack.[1] It is good to have seen something on this and many other occasions, sometimes alone, sometimes in company, of the secret of the sea and the lessons of the land from Scilly to Skye; from the Land's End to Dover; from the Nore to the Moray Firth; from Dartmoor to Lochaber; and from the Weald of Sussex to those Northumbrian lakes that lie, lonely and rather uncanny, under the Roman Wall. It is good to have attended evening chapel at Oxford, then gone up to town and danced all night (the maximum of dances with the minimum of partners), returning next morning and attending chapel again. It is good to have prevented an editor, some time before Pigott caught the *Times*, from engaging in negotiations with that ingenious person as he had intended to do; and to have actually silenced a Radical canvasser.[2] It is good

[1] I do not mention this as anything wonderful in itself, though Lord Roberts did once tell me (with his usual amiability, and perhaps thinking mainly of the boots) that a general, everyone of whose men could do as much, would be uncommonly lucky. I only say it is good to have done it.

[2] He wanted my vote, and when I told him that I was 'over the way' he politely requested leave to put some reasons on his side before me. I said, 'My good sir, I have been a political journalist for twenty years, and a student of politics and history for about thirty. I can tell you beforehand everything you are going to say, and everything I am going to answer; and your replies and so on. We are, I suppose, both busy men; can't we as well leave it where it

to have been always like-minded with the old and
not the modern law of England, to the effect that
'collective bargaining' can never be anything but
collective bullying. It is good to have read Walz's
Rhetores Graeci, and the *Grand Cyrus*, and nearly all
the English poets that anybody has ever heard of;
also to find *The Earthly Paradise*, at a twentieth
reading in 1920, as delightful as it was at a first in
1868. It is good to have heard Sims Reeves flood
St. James's Hall with 'Adelaida,' till you felt as if
you were being drowned, not in a bath but in an
ocean of musical malmsey; and to have des-
canted on the beauties of your first Burne-Jones,
without knowing that a half-puzzled, half-
amused don stood behind you. Many other things
past, and some present, have been and are—for
anything, once more, that has been is—good.

But I do not feel the slightest shame in ranking as
good likewise and very good, those voyages to the
Oracle of the Bottle and those obediences to its
utterance, taken literally as well as allegorically,
which are partially chronicled here. If I subjoin a
few examples of *menus*,[1] and some wine-lists, it is
chiefly for the purpose of illustrating the doctrines
laid down and the practices recommended in this

---

is?' He must have been better than his creed; for he smiled and
said, 'Perhaps so, sir,' and went. I should have liked to offer him
something to drink—whence the relevance here—but this
would have offended the Nonconformist Conscience and might
even have been construed into a Corrupt Practice.

[1] I do not enter into any controversy as to some points in these
menus, such as the mixture of English and French titles, and the
omission of the definite article in the latter. I do as I like, and
others may do as they like.

book. They are all records of meals and wines discussed in my own houses, and mostly devised by ourselves. Some great authorities have pronounced such things not bad reading, Barmecidal as they are. I know that I found them comfortable in the days of rationing, when there were other calls, even on the absurd modicum of meat that was allotted to one in common with babies, dead men and vegetarians, and when one had to be content with sprats and spaghetti. I wish I could imitate the Barmecide himself in following up these ghostly banquets with real ones. But I hope that all good men and all fair ladies who read me will accept the assurance that I would if I could minister unto them, even as I was privileged to do to others of their kind from fifty to five years ago, when 'we drank it as the Fates ordained it,' and took, as cheerfully as we drank it, what else the Fates ordained.

Let us begin with two specimens of a kind of dinner which I now think over-elaborated. Two *entrées* are quite enough. But the fact was that at the time when they and others like them were given (the opening years of the Cellar-Book, 1884–6), both my wife and I were rather fascinated by a French *chef* named Grégoire, who in those days both sent out and superintended dishes, less impossibly than poor Rosa Timmins's volunteer assistant, and very admirably. Alas! he died. His soufflés were sublime.[1]

---

[1] By one of these may hang a little tale. At a dinner of the usual 'sonnet' or 'fourteener' number, the lady on my left refused it; the man next her, who was busy talking to his other neighbour, did ditto; so did his accomplice; and what a seventeeth-century Puritan pamphleteer, picturesquely anticipating later slang, calls 'a rot among the Bishops,' set in. My wife might have stopped it, but didn't: and the dish came back to me virgin. I helped myself, observed gravely 'I'm sorry to keep you all waiting,' and ate. Thereupon my lady said 'It looks very good: may I change my mind?' And the man next her changed *his* mind; and his damsel followed; and they all followed — the whole dozen of them (omitting my wife, who is sometimes *propositi tenax*). I said nothing aloud: but murmured to myself and the *soufflé*, 'Sheep!'

I.

Montilla.	Consommé aux Pointes d'Asperges.
――	――
Johannisberg. Claus Auslese, 1874.	John Dory. Sauce Livournaise.
――	――
Ch. Grillet, 1865.	Filets de Saumon à la gelée.
――	――
Champagne. Jeroboam.[1] Dagonet, 1874.	Côtelettes à la Joncourt.
	――
	Plovers' Eggs.
Romanée Conti, 1858.	Aspic de Volaille à la Reine.
――	――
Ch. Margaux, 1868.	Haunch of Mutton.
	――
	Mayonnaise de Homard.
Port, 1853.	――
――	Soufflé glacé au Marasquin.
Pedro Ximénès.	――
	Canapés de Crevettes.

[1] We used to wreathe the jeroboams as centre-pieces, and a poetical guest once besought leave to crown my wife with the circlet of primroses and violets.

II.

Sherry.
'Margarita.'

———

Ch. Grillet, 1865.

———

Champagne.
St. Marceaux, 1880.

———

Ch. Latour, 1870.

———

Romanée Conti, 1858.

———

Hermitage, 1846.[1]

Consommé.

———

Filets de Sole à la
Venitienne.

———

Bastions d'Anguilles.

———

Vol au vent à la
Financière.

———

Filets de Pigeons à la
Pompadour.

———

Braised Fillet of Beef.

———

Roast Pheasants.

———

Soufflé glacé aux
Pistaches.

———

Œufs à l'Annécy.

[1] The last bottle of that spoken of in Chap. 1.

III.

As a contrast of simplicity take the following, long afterwards (some twenty years) constructed as an endeavour to carry out, for a single guest, the admirable combination of *ordre et largeur* in Foker's prescription, 'a bottle of sherry, a bottle of sham, a bottle of port, and a shass-caffy.'

Sherry.	Clear Soup.
'Titania.'	————
	Fried Trout.
————	————
Champagne.	Filets de Bœuf à la
Moët, 1893.	St. Aubyn.
	————
————	Roast Duckling.
	————
Port.	Apricots à la Rosebery.
Cockburn's 1881.	————
	Sardines
————	Dieu-sait-Comment.[1]
	————
Green Chartreuse.	Coffee.

[1] A prescription of my wife's, named by me.

IV.[1]

White Dry Paxarette.

———

White Hermitage,
1865.

———

Champagne.
Perrier-Jouet, 1884.

———

Ch. Latour, 1878.

———

Port, 1858.

———

Sherry.
Caveza.

Consommé.

———

Filets de Soles en
Crêpes.

———

Pain de Volaille.

———

Savoury Aspic.

———

Haunch of Mutton.

———

Pintades au Cresson.

———

Surprise Pudding.
Italian Cream.

———

Royans à la Bordelaise.

[1] The dinner referred to at the end of Chap. II. Date, 1894.

V.

(A dinner without champagne.)

Montilla.	Oysters.
———	———
Ch. Yquem, 1870.	Consommé.
———	———
	Grilled Red Mullet.
Ch. Margaux, 1870	———
(Magnum).	Cutlets à l'Américaine.
———	———
	Grouse.
Port.	———
Cockburn's, 1851	Macaroni Pudding.
(Magnum).	———
	Shrimp Toast.

VI.

(A June-Eating.[1])

Margarita Sherry.	Oxtail Soup.
———	———
	Whitebait.
Champagne. St. Marceaux, 1874.	———
	Mutton Cutlets.
———	———
	Chicken Salad.
Ch. Mouton-Rothschild, 1875 (Magnum).	———
	Iced Gooseberry Fool.
	———
	Olives au Nid.

[1] This was the dinner at which M. Beljame was present (see Chap. IV.). I arranged it with nothing French except the wine and the 'savoury,' on the principles of an excellent retort which my friend Mowbray Morris told me against himself. He was entertaining the famous caricaturist, Pellegrini, and half in jest (they were in London) asked if he would have some macaroni. Pellegrini shook his finger in front of his face and said: 'Mor*riss*!—my friend!— when I ask you to dinner at Naples I will not give you a beef-steak!'

VII.[1]

Sherry.	Clear Soup.
Margarita.[2]	———
———	Fillets of Whiting.
Ch. Carbonnieux, 1899.	Dutch Sauce.
———	———
Champagne.	Chicken Rissoles.
Vve. Clicquot, 1899	———
———	Saddle of Mutton.
Ch. Montrose, 1893.	———
———	Raspberry Sponge.
Port.	———
Dow's 1890.	Celery Cream.

[1] Another yoking (again many years later, for the Beljame feast was in 1886, and this in 1908) of plain home food and good foreign wine.

[2] I have said in the text that this admirable pale dry sherry was one of my greatest stand-bys all through, which will account for its frequent appearance, even in this selection.

VIII.[1]

Tio Pepe.	Consommé
————	————
Meursault, 1870.	Grilse.
————	————
	Filets de Soles Ravigotte.
Champagne.	————
Pommery.	Côtelettes de Mouton
Extra Sec, 1876.	Soubise.
————	————
Still Red Verzenay,	Chaudfroid de Volaille.
1868.	————
	Vol-au-vent Financière.
————	————
Gold Dry Sherry.	Virginian Quails.
	————
————	Soufflé glacé au Chocolat.
Ch. Lafite, 1862.	————
	Canapés d'Anchois au
	Fromage.

[1] An early (1884), and I think not bad dinner, particularly as regards the wine, though the Claret might have been better. Perhaps the chaudfroid (or chau*ffroix*, if any one prefers it), and the vol-au-vent come, in both senses, too close together. But I remember how good the still red Verzenay was with the Virginian Quails. I have spoken of the Tio Pepe and the Meursault in the text, but not, I think, of the 'Gold Dry.' It was one of Messrs. Harvey's wines, and 'of a noble race,' like Shenkin.

IX.[1]

Pale Sherry.	Clear Soup.
⎯⎯	⎯⎯
Graves, 1893.	Filleted Sole.
⎯⎯	⎯⎯
Champagne.	Dutch Sweet-breads.
Perrier Jouet, 1893.	⎯⎯
⎯⎯	Mutton Cutlets à la
Ch. Léoville-Poyferré,	Oporto.
1896.	⎯⎯
⎯⎯	Beans and Bacon.
Ch. Latour, 1893.	⎯⎯
⎯⎯	Beehive Pudding.
Port.	⎯⎯
Warre's 1884.	Cheese Trifles.

[1] 1904. Another contrast.

156

X.[1]

Vino de Pasto.	Clear Soup.
	Boiled Salmon.
	Pollo con Arroz.
Champagne. St. Marceaux, 1880.	Lobster au Gratin.
	Forequarter of Lamb.
Ch. Léoville Barton, 1874.	Cherry Tart. Meringues.
	Schabzieger Toast.

[1] A country dinner in 1888. The savoury substituted from another of the same class and time. We were very fond of Schabzieger (or -züger, for there are opposing theories), and were seldom without it. 'I hold in my soul,' as the Spanish folk-song says, two *stories* about it. In very early days my dear mother, to whose house I had brought some, implored me to 'put it out of the window.' And later, when I was buying it at Fortnum and Mason's, the aged shopman looked at me doubtfully and said, 'Excuse me, Sir, but are you acquainted with this cheese?' I assured him that this cheese and I were on the best terms. 'Oh! well, Sir,' he added, 'then I hope you'll pardon me. But only yesterday a lady came here and threw it on the counter and said, "Young man [N.B. He must have been at least 80], what do you mean by selling stuff like this?" So I said, 'Please, ma'am, how did you eat it?' and *she* said, "Why of course like any other cheese; we cut it in pieces and *tried* to eat it!!!" ' The elect need not be informed that it should be grated, mixed with butter, and spread, not too lavishly, on toast. As for its

In coming to some specimens, few out of many, of dinners given in that most hospitable of places, Edinburgh, there is a touch of sadness in the sifting. Naturally enough, our hosts to begin with, and guests afterwards, were, as a rule, older people than in earlier days: and in looking over the lists jotted on the backs of the cards (not, as some cynic puts it, to signify 'paid off,' but to prevent repetition of just the same company another time), I have sometimes found that all except ourselves have joined the majority. The last dinner (XV.) is that at which our Finnish Venus (*v. sup.* p. 55) drank and liked the '74 Sauterne. Shortly after this, domestic reasons made us give up going out to dinner, and entertaining, except on a small scale, and very rarely on a larger, at home.

---

odour, some Cypriote cheese, which the arbitrary but beneficent Jubal Webb (known formerly to all dwellers in or near Kensington) let me have as a favour, could give it twenty in fifty and beat it. This was a light on some mentions of cheese in Greek literature: though I was never man enough to try it with Greek *wine*, not being, as above observed, Hercules. I should like to draw attention to the 'Pollo con Arroz,' an excellent Spanish dish which I found in one of the 96 cookery books I once possessed, and never saw elsewhere till the other day at the Old University Club in Suffolk Street, where a good friend (not for the first time by many) guested me.

XI.

White Dry Paxarette.	Consommé.
——	——
Montrachet.	Cod. Green Dutch Sauce.
——	——
Champagne.	Centres de Limandes.
Dagonet.	——
Brut, 1887.	Mutton Cutlets aux Pastèques.
——	——
Port, 1858.	Chicken Salad.
——	——
Romanée, 1887.	Ecrevisses à la Crême.
——	——
Ch. Léoville, 1878.	Boiled Turkey.
——	——
Golden Sherry.	Haunch of Venison.
	——
	Pears with Apple Sauce.
	——
	Plum Pudding.
	Chocolate Cream.
	——
	Saumon Panaché.

XII.

Amontillado.	Consommé.
———	———
Hock.	Soles à la Stamford.
Deidesheimer, 1886.	———
	Escalopes de Veau.
	Sauce Génoise.
———	———
Champagne.	Canapés Tria-juncta.[1]
Moët, 1889.	———
	Saddle of Mutton.
———	———
	Capercailzie with
Romanée, 1887.	Cranberry Sauce.
	———
———	Macédoine au
	Champagne.
Ch. Léoville, 1878.[2]	———
	Chocolate Meringues.
———	———
Port, 1873;	Salmagundy.
bòtt. 1882.	———
	Ices.

[1] This was a device of my own, I believe, but I forget what the three things were.

[2] I have never drunk a bad Léoville (Barton at least, for though Lascases and Poyferré—see Menu IX., one of the few good wines

XIII.

Sherry. Dos Cortados, 1873.	Clear Soup.
—	Fillets of Whiting.
Ch. La Frette, 1865.	Calf's Head à la Terrapin.
—	Oysters en caisses.
Champagne. Giesler, 1889.	Aspic of Tunny.
—	Braised Beef.
Ch. Margaux, 1870.	Roast Guinea Fowls.
—	Apricots in Jelly.
Burgundy. La Tâche, 1886.	Velvet Cream.
—	Anchois Zadioff.
Port, 1870.	Ices.

of its year—can be excellent, they are less immutable), just as I have never smoked a bad Flor de Cuba; but I do not say that I have never drunk a better wine than the one or smoked a better cigar than the other.

XIV.

Sherry.	Clear Soup.
'Isabel,' 1868.	——
	Beignets of Halibut.
——	——
	Vol-au-vent de Homard.
Scharzhofberger, 1893.	——
	Reform Cutlets.
——	——
Champagne.	Boiled Turkey.
Irroy, 1893.	——
	Blackcock.[1]
——	——
	Viennese Pudding.
Ch. de Beychevelle, 1878	——
(magnum).	Meringue Anonyme.
	——
——	Sardines à la Titania.
	——
Port, 1872.	Ices.

[1] On seeing this in print my wife said (and I agree with her) that we might have improved the combination of turkey and blackcock.

XV.

Golden Sherry.	Clear Soup.
—	—
Sauterne, 1874.	Zootje of Sole.
—	—
Champagne.	Mutton Cutlets.
Perrier-Jouet, 1893.	—
	Eggs in Cream Sauce.
—	—
Ch. Lafite-Carruades,	Boiled Chicken.
1878.	—
	Ham and Peas.
—	—
Port.	Easter Pudding.
Graham's 1881.	—
	Risotto en caisses.

POSTSCRIPTS

(1) Unconfessed injustice is only worthy of a teetotaller. I see I have omitted that most excellent creature, shandygaff, one of the rare cases of thoroughly successful coalition. And, in a certain limitation (p. 27) of my praise of Feuerheerd's Port. I had forgotten that the admirable late-bottled '73, which I have celebrated in the context, was, almost certainly, that shipper's. Another omission, though not one involving injustice, was in the list of bottle-sizes — that of the imperial *quart*. It is uncommon but useful, and I once had some champagne (Giesler) in it.

(2) The Budget has just paid a fresh and flattering, if inconvenient, compliment to the patriotism of good drinkers.

(3) I cannot help quoting, as a colophon to this little book, some memorable words of Professor H. E. Armstrong's in a recent letter to the *Times* about synthetic and natural indigo. He closed with a parallel. Alcohol as alcohol could be obtained, he said, from all sorts of things; not so 'a vintage wine, one of the most perfect of nature's products — to those who can appreciate perfection.' And it is so. On those who would deprive us of it, let the curse of Nature rest.

G. S.,
1 Royal Crescent, Bath,
St. George's Day, 1920.

GEORGE SAINTSBURY[1]

Seldom does so ripe and so full a scholar and
man leave the world of good books and compan-
ionable wine as the veteran George Saintsbury,
who has just died in the Augustan peace of the
Royal Crescent at Bath. It was a sound instinct
that led him to choose that stately habitation as
the residence of his old age. For here was a man
cast altogether in a mightier mould than most
professors and students of literature; who enjoyed
life up to the last, had read and remembered
everything worth reading, read many things
many times over with fresh zest every time, and
written with a wisdom, a relish, and a point of
view all his own. If the 'lives of the scholars' were
a recognized institution like those of the saints,
George Saintsbury would certainly have to have
his place among them. They would include not

165

too many like him, and there would perhaps be some surprising exclusions—heads learned enough, but heads whose learning depressed them. To be able to rise out of the welter of universal reading on steady legs, and with 'courage and the upward countenance', to use Saintsbury's own words, is given to few, though as business with literature is at bottom a human business the vitality of the trafficker in it is in the last resort decisive.

For this reason to weigh the judgments in Saintsbury's numerous writings, or in Johnson's, as a chemist might weigh substances, is beside the point. The main thing about heroes of this build is their individuality. If it is thought that there is something after all rather easy-going in a life of perpetual literary enjoyment, it must be borne in mind that if it is to be led honestly and fruitfully, as Saintsbury's was, it is bound also to have its pains, hidden though they may be. A famous, even hackneyed, passage in Dante—a favourite with another heroic scholar, the late W. P. Ker— bids men remember that they are formed, not to live like brutes, but to 'follow virtue and knowledge.' This justification of the scholar's life was quoted once with fine effect by one of the first critics of the age, still with us. His scriptural addition to it, though addressed to a young audience, is worth recalling in memory of the magnanimous man of encyclopaedic studies now departed:—'He that refuseth instruction despiseth his own soul.'